THE
STUDENT
LEADERSHIP
CHALLENGE

Also by James M. Kouzes and Barry Z. Posner

Student Leadership Practices Inventory (SLPI)

Student Leadership Practices Inventory: Student Workbook

Student Leadership Practices Inventory: Facilitator's Guide

Student Leadership Practices Inventory Online

Student Leadership Planner: An Action Guide to Achieving Your Personal Best

The Jossey-Bass Academic Administrator's Guide to Exemplary Leadership

THE
STUDENT
LEADERSHIP
CHALLENGE

FIVE PRACTICES FOR EXEMPLARY LEADERS

JAMES M. KOUZES
and
BARRY Z. POSNER

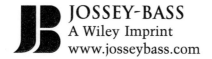
JOSSEY-BASS
A Wiley Imprint
www.josseybass.com

Published by Jossey-Bass
A Wiley Imprint
989 Market Street, San Francisco, CA 94103-1741—www.josseybass.com

The Five Practices of Exemplary Leadership® and The Five Practices of Exemplary Student Leadership® are registered trademarks of J.M. Kouzes and B.Z. Posner.

Martin Luther King Jr.'s "I Have a Dream" speech © 1963 Dr. Martin Luther King, Jr; copyright renewed Coretta Scott King, 1991.

Readers should be aware that Internet Web sites offered as citations and/or sources for further information may have changed or disappeared between the time this was written and when it is read.

Limit of Liability/Disclaimer of Warranty: While the publisher and author have used their best efforts in preparing this book, they make no representations or warranties with respect to the accuracy or completeness of the contents of this book and specifically disclaim any implied warranties of merchantability or fitness for a particular purpose. No warranty may be created or extended by sales representatives or written sales materials. The advice and strategies contained herein may not be suitable for your situation. You should consult with a professional where appropriate. Neither the publisher nor author shall be liable for any loss of profit or any other commercial damages, including but not limited to special, incidental, consequential, or other damages.

Jossey-Bass books and products are available through most bookstores. To contact Jossey-Bass directly call our Customer Care Department within the U.S. at 800-956-7739, outside the U.S. at 317-572-3986, or fax 317-572-4002.

Jossey-Bass also publishes its books in a variety of electronic formats. Some content that appears in print may not be available in electronic books.

Library of Congress Cataloging-in-Publication Data

Kouzes, James M., 1945–
    The student leadership challenge : five practices for exemplary leaders / James M. Kouzes and Barry Z. Posner.
        p. cm.
    Includes index.
    ISBN 978-0-470-17705-1 (pbk.)
    1. College student government. 2. Leadership. I. Posner, Barry Z. II. Title.
    LB2346.K68 2008
    378.1'98—dc22

                                                                        2008016485

Printed in the United States of America
FIRST EDITION
PB Printing 10 9 8 7 6 5 4 3 2 1

CONTENTS

THE
STUDENT
LEADERSHIP
CHALLENGE

INTRODUCTION: GETTING EXTRAORDINARY THINGS DONE IN ORGANIZATIONS

The Student Leadership Challenge is about how student leaders *mobilize others to want to get extraordinary things done* in organizations. It's about the practices they use to transform values into actions, visions into realities, obstacles into innovations, separateness into solidarity, and risks into rewards. It's about leadership that creates the climate in which challenging opportunities are transformed into remarkable successes.

There are no shortages of challenging opportunities. Although in these extraordinary times the challenges seem only to be increasing in number and complexity, all generations confront their own serious threats and receive their own favorable circumstances. The abundance of challenges, however, is not the issue; it's how you respond to them that matters. Through your responses you have the potential to either seriously worsen or profoundly improve the world in which you live, study, and work.

The most significant contribution student leaders make is not simply to today's issues and goals but rather to the long-term development of people, communities, and institutions so they can adapt, change, prosper, and grow. The domain of leaders is the future, and leadership is not the private reserve of a few charismatic men and women. It is a process ordinary people use when they are bringing forth the best from themselves and others. When the leader in everyone is liberated, extraordinary things happen.

Leadership is a process. It is a journey, not a single destination, and the conclusion of any successful (even extraordinary) endeavor is simply the beginning point for the next adventure. Meeting the leadership challenge is a personal—and a daily—challenge for all of us. In the final analysis, leadership development is self-development. We know that if you have the will and the way to lead, you can. You have to supply the will. *The Student Leadership Challenge* will supply the way.

YOU MAKE A DIFFERENCE

The fundamental purpose of *The Student Leadership Challenge* is to assist students—whether in a formal or official leadership position or not—in furthering their abilities to lead others to get extraordinary things done. You are capable of developing yourself as a leader far more than tradition has ever assumed possible.

> *Some people make things happen,*
>
> *some watch things happen, while others*
>
> *wonder what has happened.*
>
> —Gaelic proverb

Our findings from the analysis of thousands of personal-best leadership case studies challenge the myth that leadership is something that you find only at the highest levels of organizations and society. We found it everywhere. These findings also challenge the belief that leadership is reserved for only a handful of very special people. Leadership is not a gene or an inheritance. Leadership is an identifiable set of skills and abilities that are available to everyone. The "great person" theory of leadership is just plain wrong. Or, we should say, the theory that there are only a few select men and women who can lead others to greatness is just plain wrong.

Another notion that is plain wrong is that leaders come only from large, or great, or small, or breakthrough organizations, or from established economies, or from start-up companies. They come from anywhere and everywhere. We consider the male and female students in our research to be exemplary leaders, and so do those with whom they worked, even though the vast majority of them aren't known outside of their colleges or communities. They are the everyday heroes of our world. It's because there are so many—not so few—student leaders that extraordinary things get done on a regular basis, especially in extraordinary times.

The Student Leadership Challenge is written both to strengthen your abilities and to uplift your spirits. We intend it to be practical and inspirational. We also make you a promise: Everything in this book is evidence-based. Everything we write about, everything we advise is solidly based in research—our own and others'. If you engage in the practices we describe in this book, you will improve your performance and the performance of your team. There is a catch, of course. You have to do it with commitment and consistency. Excellence in anything—whether it's leadership, music, sports, or academics—requires disciplined practice.

> *Practice is the best of all instructors.*
>
> —Pubilius Syrus

This book has its origins in a research project we began over twenty-five years ago. We wanted to know what people did—from teenagers to executives to senior citizens, from the campus to the corner office, from Main Street to Tiananmen Square—when they were at their "personal best" in leading others. The personal bests were experiences in which our study respondents, in their own estimation, set their individual leadership standards of excellence. We started with an assumption that we didn't have to interview and survey star performers or top executives in excellent companies to discover best practices. Instead, we assumed that by asking regular people to describe extraordinary leadership experiences we would find patterns of success. And we did.

We repeated this research with student leaders, and we found exactly the same thing. When they are doing their best, student leaders exhibit an identifiable set of practices, which vary little from campus to campus—whether small or large, public or private, northern or southern, rural or urban—or even from community to community and country to country. Good leadership is an understandable and universal process. Though each student leader is a unique individual, there are shared patterns to the practice of leadership. And these practices can be learned.

This book is about how college students exercise leadership at its best. The stories you will read are the real-life experiences of regular students,

> *The formula for success is simple:*
> *practice and concentration, then more*
> *practice and more concentration.*
>
> —Babe Didrikson Zaharias

from all walks of life—people like you—who get bigger-than-life results.* This is not a book about famous people or about people in positions of high power—although we have peppered the text with short quotations from such people in a variety of fields to give you a look at leadership through some different lenses. It's a book about students who have the courage and spirit to make a significant difference.

One of the most dangerous and irresponsible myths about leadership is that it is the province of just a handful of people, a magical ability reserved for the unique individuals of fairy tales or science fiction novels. Leadership is not something mysterious, mystical, or ethereal that cannot be understood, learned, and practiced by ordinary people. It is a myth that only a lucky few can decipher the leadership code. You have within you the ability to accept and embrace the leadership challenge to make a difference, because it is who you are and what you do that matters.

A FIELD GUIDE FOR LEADERS

The student leaders we've worked with and learned from have asked us many questions about enhancing their leadership capabilities. In *The*

---

* Unless otherwise noted, all student stories, examples, and quotations are taken from personal interviews and correspondence or from personal-best leadership case studies written by student leaders during or shortly after their college careers. In reporting their leadership experiences, we do not specify their school or location because The Five Practices of Exemplary Leadership hold true for the complete range of campus environments—large and small, private and public, urban and rural—in the United States and abroad.

Student Leadership Challenge, we offer guidance on these and other questions:

- What beliefs and values guide my actions as a leader?
- What is the source of self-confidence required to lead others?
- How do I best set an example for others?
- How do I articulate a vision of the future when things are so unpredictable?
- How do I improve my ability to get people excited?
- How do I create an environment that promotes innovation and risk?
- How do I build a cohesive and spirited team?
- How do I share power and information and still maintain accountability?
- How do I put more joy and celebration into our efforts?
- How do I improve my leadership abilities?

Think of *The Student Leadership Challenge* as a field guide to take along on your leadership journey. You begin the expedition with this chapter and the next. This introduction gives you a point of view about leadership; Chapter Two provides an overview of The Five Practices of Exemplary Leadership® revealed in our research. Chapters Three through Seven explore The Five Practices in depth. We have designed each of those chapters to describe one leadership practice and explain the essential behaviors that student leaders employ to get extraordinary things done (what we refer to as The Ten Commitments of Leadership). We offer evidence from our research, and that of others, to support the practices and commitments, recount actual case examples of real students who demonstrate each practice, and prescribe specific recommendations on what you can do to make each practice your own and to continue your development as a leader.

> *It's what you learn after you know it all that counts.*
>
> —John Wooden

Along the way we suggest steps to take, alone or with others, to build specific skills in becoming a better leader. Each of our suggestions is a "small win." Whether the focus is your own learning or the development of your constituents you can take immediate action on every one of the recommendations. They require little or no budget; they don't need any elaborate or extensive discussions, consensus among peers, or approval of some professor, faculty advisor, or college administrator. They just require your personal commitment and discipline.

The closing chapter sounds a call to action, a call to everyone to accept personal responsibility to be a role model for leadership. Among the recurring lessons from the research is this: leadership is everyone's business, and the first place to look for leadership is within yourself. The closing chapter asks you to consider the difference you want to make, the legacy you want to leave. And when you read to the very end of this book, the secret to success in life will be revealed.

THE FIVE PRACTICES OF EXEMPLARY LEADERSHIP

As we've conducted research on personal-best leadership experiences over the years, we've discovered countless examples of how student leaders mobilize others to get extraordinary things done in virtually every arena of organized activity. We've found them in student government, fraternities and sororities, dorms and residential learning communities, collegiate and intramural sports, multicultural centers, ROTC, campus ministry, student unions, community service, clubs, and classroom projects. Student leaders reside in every campus, in every city and every country, in every position and every place. They're employees, volunteers, classmates, teammates; they're women and men, young and old, of every creed and nationality. Leadership knows no racial or religious bounds, no ethnic or cultural borders. Exemplary leadership can be found everywhere you look.

From our analysis of thousands of personal-best leadership experiences, we've discovered that people who guide others along pioneering journeys follow rather similar paths. Though each experience we examined was unique in expression, all the cases followed remarkably similar patterns of action in a wide range of settings. We've forged these common practices into a model of leadership, and we offer it here as guidance for students as they attempt to keep their own bearings as leaders and steer others toward peak achievements.

As we looked deeper into the dynamic process of leadership, through case analyses and survey questionnaires, we uncovered five practices common to students' personal-best leadership experiences. When getting extraordinary things done in organizations, student leaders engage in these Five Practices of Exemplary Leadership:

- Model the Way
- Inspire a Shared Vision
- Challenge the Process
- Enable Others to Act
- Encourage the Heart

The Five Practices—which we preview in this chapter and then discuss in depth in Chapters Three through Seven—aren't the private property of the students we studied or of a few select shining stars. Leadership is not about personality; it's about behavior. The Five Practices are available to anyone who accepts the leadership challenge. And they're also not the accident of a particular time; as the most recent research confirms, they're just as relevant today as they have been in the past.

MODEL THE WAY

Titles are granted, but it's your behavior that wins you respect. As Neil Kucera told us, "Leadership is mostly the model you provide for your peers in how you behave." When his service organization accepted responsibility for working with a group of at-risk adolescents, he explained that "we seldom told the kids how to behave—we simply showed them an example, and it was contagious. The kids were always watching us, studying how we acted, looking up to us, and wanting to mimic our behavior." This sentiment was shared across all the cases that we collected. Exemplary student leaders know that if they want to gain commitment and reach the highest standards, they must be models of the behavior they expect of others. Leaders *model the way.*

To effectively model the behavior they expect of others, student leaders must first be clear about their own guiding principles. They must *clarify values.* Jason Ting explained that when he was elected president of his student organization, "I had to figure out for myself, and within myself, what I thought was important and why. Then I needed to make certain that what I was doing was consistent with these values and standards." Student leaders like Jason must dig deep inside to figure out their values, and then they must clearly and distinctly give voice to them. As the personal-best stories illustrate, student leaders are supposed to stand up for their beliefs, so they'd better have some beliefs to stand up for. But it's not just the leaders' values that are important. Leaders aren't just representing themselves. They speak and act on behalf of a larger community. They must build agreement around common principles and common ideals.

Eloquent speeches about common values, however, aren't nearly enough. Deeds are far more important than words when others want to determine how serious you really are about what you say. Words and deeds must be consistent. Exemplary student leaders *set the example* through daily actions that demonstrate they are deeply committed to their beliefs. "I would never ask my teammates to do something I wouldn't be willing to do myself," Wesley Lord reported. "They knew that if I asked them for something that I would be willing to do the same if they asked me." Mark Almassy echoed this same insight. As captain of the volleyball team, he said, "I always showed up early to practice and oftentimes stayed late. There was nothing I wasn't willing to do. I was not too good to mop the floor or too cool to shout words of encouragement to a freshman." Student leaders understand that actions speak louder than words, and, as Mark puts it, "I made sure to show people what to do rather than tell them what to do."

> **We must become the change we want to see.**
>
> —Mahatma Ghandi

The personal-best projects we heard about were all distinguished by relentless effort, steadfastness, competence, and attention to detail. We were also struck by how the actions that student leaders took to set an example were often simple things. Sure, they had plans, but the examples they gave were not about elaborate designs. They were about the power of spending time with someone, of working side by side with colleagues, of sharing a laugh or even a tear, of telling stories that made values come alive, of being highly visible during times of uncertainty, and of asking questions to get people to think about values and priorities. Model the Way is about earning the right and the respect to lead through direct involvement and action. Students follow first the person, then the plan.

INSPIRE A SHARED VISION

When students described to us their personal-best leadership experiences, they told of times when they imagined an exciting, highly attractive future for their group, team, or organization. They had visions and dreams of what *could* be. They had absolute and total personal belief in those dreams, and they were confident in their abilities to make extraordinary things happen. Every project, every organization, every social movement begins with a dream. The dream or vision is the force that invents the future. Leaders *inspire a shared vision.* As John Irby explained from his own personal-best leadership experience, "Inspiring others to envision their success and giving them an image of what that would look like injects drive and determination into those around you."

> *The very essence of leadership is [that]*
> *you have a vision. It's got to be a vision you*
> *articulate clearly and forcefully on every occasion.*
> *You can't blow an uncertain trumpet.*
>
> —Theodore Hesburgh

Student leaders gaze across the horizon of time, imagining the attractive opportunities that are in store for the time when they and their constituents arrive at a distant destination. They *envision the future,* the exciting and ennobling possibilities ahead. They have a desire to make something happen, to change the way things are, to create something that no one else has ever created before. In some ways, student leaders live their lives backward. They see pictures in their mind's eye of what the results will look like even before they've started their project, much as an architect draws a blueprint or an engineer builds a model. Their clear image of the future pulls them forward. Yet visions seen only by leaders are insufficient to create an organized movement or a significant change on a campus or in the community. A person with no constituents is not a leader, and people will not follow until they accept a vision as their own. Leaders cannot command commitment, they can only inspire it.

Student leaders have to *enlist others* in a common vision. To enlist people in a vision, you must get to know your constituents and speak their language. People must believe that you understand their needs and have their interests at heart. Leadership is a dialogue, not a monologue. To enlist support, you must have intimate knowledge of people's dreams, hopes, aspirations, and values.

What may begin as "my" vision emerges as "our" vision. This is precisely what Zeebah Aleshi learned when serving as first chair in her school's wind ensemble band. When their band director suffered a sudden illness and was gone for months, the majority of the band members grew apathetic toward music and practicing. Zeebah said she wasn't about to sit back and watch her fellow band members fling away what they had once been passionate about: "I talked with each of them and showed them how our band was not just important to me; it was important to all of us and the school. I made them realize they were throwing away their love and passion for music. I helped them find the reason why they were sitting in the band seats and why they were here; we were all here to create music; music so beautiful that would cause our friends, parents, and teacher to have tears rolling down their cheeks. Music was not our only passion, but it was part of who we were, and together we could accomplish so much more."

Student leaders breathe life into the hopes and dreams of others and enable them to see the exciting possibilities that the future holds. They forge a unity of purpose by showing constituents how the dream is for the common good. Leaders stir the fire of passion in others by expressing enthusiasm for the compelling vision of their group. Whatever the venue, and without exception, the students we've studied reported that they were incredibly enthusiastic about their personal-best projects. Their own enthusiasm was catching; it spread from them to their constituents. Belief in the vision and enthusiasm for it are the sparks that ignite the flame of inspiration.

CHALLENGE THE PROCESS

Every single personal-best leadership case involved some kind of challenge. The challenge might have been turning around a losing season or failed rush program, starting a new club, designing an honor code, revamping residential hall policies, constructing an invigorating campaign to get adolescents to join an environmental program, winning a case competition, or launching a new program, product, or service. Whatever the challenge, all the personal-best experiences involved a departure from the status quo. Not one student claimed to have achieved a personal best by keeping things the same. All leaders *challenge the process.*

The work of student leaders is change, and they are always on the lookout for ways that things could be better than they are; they don't sit idly by waiting for fate or fortune to smile on them. "Luck" or "being in the right place at the right time" may play a role in the specific opportunities leaders embrace, but those who lead others to greatness seek and accept challenge. In describing her personal-best leadership experience, Patricia Hua told us, "No one else seemed willing to try and make our idea work, because everyone thought that the chances of success were too slim and hence not worth the time and energy. But I thought that we could do something that had never been done before. It was always *possible.*" Patricia was constantly looking around for ways to improve their team, finding ways to stay current about what others were doing, and taking the initiative to try new things.

Leaders are pioneers. They are willing to step out into the unknown. They *search for opportunities to innovate, grow, and improve.* But student leaders aren't the only creators or originators of new products, services, or processes. In fact, it's more likely that they're not; innovation comes more from listening than from telling. Student leaders have to constantly be looking outside of themselves and their organizations for new and innovative programs, processes, and services. "The process of trial and error gave me a new perspective on what is required to be a successful leader," is how Allison Avon explained it. With this new perspective, she can offer this advice: "When the process challenges you . . . challenge back! That's simply the only way that things are going to get any better."

When it comes to innovation, the major contributions of student leaders are to create a climate for experimentation, recognize good ideas, support those ideas, and be willing to challenge the system to get new programs, processes, services, and systems adopted. It might be more accurate, then, to say that leaders aren't the inventors as much as they are the early patrons and adopters of innovation.

> *Innovation distinguishes between*
> *a leader and a follower.*
>
> —Steve Jobs

Student leaders know well that innovation and change involve *experimenting and taking risks.* Despite the inevitability of mistakes and failures, they proceed anyway. One way of dealing with the potential risks and failures of experimentation is to approach change through incremental steps and small wins. Little victories, when piled on top of each other, build confidence that even the biggest challenges can be met. In the process, commitment to the long-term future is strengthened. Not everyone is equally comfortable with risk and uncertainty. You must pay attention to the capacity of your constituents to take control of challenging situations and become fully committed to change. You can't exhort people to take risks if they don't also feel safe.

> **The trouble is, if you don't risk anything, you risk even more.**
> —Erica Jong

It would be ridiculous to assert that those who fail over and over again eventually succeed as leaders. Success in any endeavor isn't a process of simply buying enough lottery tickets. The key that unlocks the door to opportunity is learning. So many student leaders, like Allison Avon, told us that "leaders are constantly learning from their errors and failures." Life is the leader's laboratory, and exemplary leaders use it to conduct as many experiments as possible. *Try, fail, and learn. Try, fail, and learn. Try, fail, and learn.* That's the leader's mantra. Student leaders are learners. You need to learn from your failures as well as your successes and to make it possible for others to do the same.

ENABLE OTHERS TO ACT

Grand dreams don't become significant realities through the actions of a single person. It requires a team effort. It requires solid trust and strong relationships. It requires deep competence and cool confidence. It requires group collaboration and individual accountability. To get extraordinary things done in organizations, student leaders have to *enable others to act.*

> *Keep away from people who belittle*
> *your ambitions. Small people always do that,*
> *but the really great make you feel*
> *that you, too, can become great.*
>
> —Mark Twain

Student leaders *foster collaboration* and build trust. This sense of teamwork goes far beyond a small circle of constituents or close confidants. You need to engage all those who must make the project work—and, in some way, all who must live with the results. Francesca Battaglia learned this the hard way, but learn it she did. Like so many student leaders, she told us, "I used to believe that 'if you want something done right, do it yourself.' I found out the hard way that this is just impossible to do. One day I was ready to just give up the position because I could no longer handle all of the work. My advisor noticed that I was overwhelmed, and she turned to me and said three magic words: *Use your committee!* The best piece of advice I would pass along about being an effective leader is that it is OK to rely on others to get the job done."

Student leaders make it possible for others to do good work. They know that those who are expected to produce the results must feel a sense of personal power and ownership. They understand that the command-and-control techniques of traditional management no longer apply. Instead, student leaders work to make people feel strong, capable, and committed. You enable others to act not by hoarding the power you have but by giving it away. Student leaders *strengthen others.* By this we mean they help everyone develop the capacity to deliver on the promises they make. As Kim Wizer learned working with her sorority sisters: "We involved everyone in the chapter, rather than just the executive officers." She made sure to seek out the opinions of all her sorority sisters and used these discussions not only to build up their capabilities but also to educate and update her own information and perspective. Kim realized that when people are trusted and have more discretion, more authority, and more information, they're much more likely to use their energies to produce extraordinary results.

> *You may be deceived if you trust*
> *too much, but you will live in torment*
> *if you do not trust enough.*
>
> —Frank Crane

In the stories and cases students shared, they proudly discussed teamwork, trust, and empowerment as essential elements of their efforts. Constituents neither perform at their best nor stick around for very long if you make them feel weak, dependent, or alienated. But when you help people feel strong and capable—as if they can do more than they ever thought possible—they'll give it their all and exceed their own expectations. Authentic leadership is founded on trust, and the more people trust their leader—and each other—the more they take risks, make changes, and keep organizations and movements alive. Through that relationship, leaders turn their constituents into leaders themselves.

ENCOURAGE THE HEART

The climb to the top is arduous and long. People become exhausted, frustrated, and disenchanted. They're often tempted to give up. Student leaders *encourage the heart* of their constituents to carry on. Genuine acts of caring uplift the spirit and draw people forward. In his personal-best leadership experience, Ken Campos told us, he had shared the feelings of being underappreciated and undervalued along with many of his coworkers, so when he became the shift supervisor he took many steps to turn around this attitude. "I would constantly extol and commend them for their actions, and more important, I tried to make it clear that we were making a difference as a team," he told us. "I looked for ways to make our work fun, and whenever anyone did something special, we all stopped to give that person a high-five or a chorus of 'way-to-go' chants."

Recognizing contributions can be one-to-one or with many people. It can come from dramatic gestures or simple actions. Kristen Cornell, as captain of her volleyball team, said she "found that encouraging my teammates was one of the easiest and most beneficial things I could do to make the team better." Extending this insight, David Braverman, in changing the culture within his residence hall, observed, "Showing that you care about someone is a simple yet overlooked quality of a leader." It's part of the leader's job to show appreciation for people's contributions and to create a culture of *celebrating values and victories.*

In the cases we've collected there are countless examples of individual recognition and group celebration. They range from handwritten thank-you notes, face-to-face tributes, and personally mixed CDs to serenades, marching bands, and firework displays. Student leaders make sure that the people they are working with are recognized for their contributions, because they want to provide a climate in which everyone feels cared about and genuinely appreciated.

> *Flatter me, and I may not believe you.*
> *Criticize me, and I may not like you.*
> *Ignore me, and I may not forgive you.*
> *Encourage me—and I may not forget you.*
>
> —William Arthur Ward

Recognition and celebration aren't about fun and games, though there is a lot of fun and there are a lot of games when student leaders encourage the hearts of their constituents. Neither are they about pretentious ceremonies designed to create some phony sense of camaraderie. Encouragement is a curiously serious business. By celebrating people's accomplishments visibly and in group settings, student leaders create and sustain a team spirit. By basing celebrations on the accomplishment of key values and milestones, they sustain focus and enhance motivation. When striving to bring about dramatic change of any kind—whether it is making an 180-degree turnaround, recovering from disaster, or starting up a new program—you must make certain that people see the benefit of behavior that's aligned with your group's goals and values. Realize that celebrations and rituals, when done with authenticity and from the heart, build a strong sense of collective identity and community spirit that can carry a group through turbulent and difficult moments.

Embedded in The Five Practices of Exemplary Leadership are behaviors that serve as the basis for learning to lead. We call these The Ten Commitments of Leadership (see Table 2.1). The Student Leadership Practices Inventory (SLPI) described in the Appendix further translates The Five Practices into behavioral statements so that students can assess their skills and use this feedback to improve their leadership abilities.

LEADERSHIP IS EVERYONE'S BUSINESS

After analyzing thousands of personal-best leadership experiences from student leaders around the globe, an additional insight emerges: *leadership is everyone's business*. Leadership is not about position or rank; rather, it is about a process that can be understood, grasped, and learned. Leadership, just like any other skill in life, can be strengthened through coaching and practice. But no amount of coaching or practice can make

TABLE 2.1 THE FIVE PRACTICES AND TEN COMMITMENTS OF LEADERSHIP.

Model the Way	1. Clarify values by finding your voice and affirming shared ideals.
	2. Set the example by aligning actions and shared values.
Inspire a Shared Vision	3. Envision the future by imagining exciting and ennobling possibilities.
	4. Enlist others in a common vision by appealing to shared aspirations.
Challenge the Process	5. Search for opportunities by seizing the initiative and by looking outward for innovative ways to improve.
	6. Experiment and take risks by constantly generating small wins and learning from experience.
Enable Others to Act	7. Foster collaboration by building trust and facilitating relationships.
	8. Strengthen others by increasing self-determination and developing competence.
Encourage the Heart	9. Recognize contributions by showing appreciation for individual excellence.
	10. Celebrate the values and victories by creating a spirit of community.

much of a difference if you don't care about doing better for yourself as well as for others. Leadership development is fundamentally self-development, and it begins with an exploration of your inner territory.

Here are some steps to start your leadership development journey.

I. MY PERSONAL-BEST EXPERIENCE OF LEADERSHIP

With leadership, as with many things in life, experience can be the best teacher. We learn what to do by trying it ourselves or by watching others. The problem is that not all of what's done or observed is effective or appropriate behavior. So it's important to base our leadership practices on the best of what people do or see—those times when people perform at their best as leaders or when we observe others at their best.

This assignment is designed to get you to focus on *your* personal-best leadership experience. You may be discussing this experience with a few others, so it's important that you complete this brief task prior to that conversation. Writing this case study about your own personal-best leadership experience can take anywhere from fifteen minutes to an hour, so please set aside adequate time for both reflection and expression.

1. Recall a time when you did your *very best* as a leader. Think about a time when you set your *individual standard of excellence* as a leader. It's a time when you *excelled.* Your leadership experience can be in school; in a classroom, club, or team; in the community, a religious group, or a sports team; or in the workplace. It can be one that you are presently involved with or one you were involved with some time in the past; in the public or private sector; as an appointed, selected, or "emerged" leader; for pay or as a volunteer. Write a very brief identifying description of that experience in the following space so you can give everyone an understanding of the context. For example: When did this occur? Who was involved? What challenges did you face?

2. Thinking about the case you just selected, what are the five to seven actions you took as a leader that made a difference? That is, what specifically would you say you did as a leader that mobilized your group or organization to get extraordinary things done?

a.

b.

c.

d.

e.

f.

g.

3. What were the two or three major lessons that you learned *about leadership* from this experience? That is, if you were going to give someone else advice about being a leader, based on your own experience, what would you tell that person?

a.

b.

c.

II. A LEADER I HAVE FOLLOWED

Your personal experiences with individuals you consider to be leaders have much to teach you about the difference that people can make in your life. You learn about leadership as you have experiences with people you admire as leaders and observe how they bring out the best in you and others.

Take a moment to think about a time when you *willingly* followed the direction of someone you admired and respected as a leader. (For

many students this person is one of their teachers, coaches, or relatives.)
Answer the following questions:

1. What was the situation (the project, program, or activity) in which
   you were involved with this person?

2. How did this person make you feel? What are the three or four
   words you would use to describe how you felt when you were
   involved with this person and how this person made you feel
   about yourself?

   a.

   b.

   c.

   d.

3. What five to seven leadership actions did this person take to get
   you and others to want to perform at your best? Think about
   what this individual did as a leader that you admired and respected, and what specifically they did as a leader that mobilized your
   group or organization to get extraordinary things done.

   a.

   b.

   c.

   d.

   e.

   f.

   g.

III. OTHER INDIVIDUALS WHOM I ADMIRE AS LEADERS, AND WHY

You have interacted with many individuals over the course of your life. Some have had considerable influence on you, others much less. Think about people you know who you would say are leaders. They don't have to be anyone that anybody else would know, and they don't need to be perfect role models.

1. Think of at least three people and make notes to yourself in the space below. What was their relationship to you? What was the context in which you knew or interacted with this person? What was it about this person and his or her actions that made you think of the person as a leader?

    a.

    b.

    c.

2. Looking over your notes about these three individuals, what five to seven key observations would you make about what the people you admire as leaders *do*? Be prepared to discuss your conclusions with others.

    a.

    b.

    c.

    d.

    e.

    f.

    g.

3

MODEL THE WAY

Michael Gibler was ecstatic when he was hired at Ultrazone, a laser tag arena and arcade that is nearly a landmark in his town.

> It seemed like the perfect job for me. . . . The people there were relaxed, kind, motivated, and really seemed to enjoy their work. The pay was lower than other jobs I had been offered, but the scheduling was flexible and the commute was short so I could walk to work. Like I said, it was near perfect.

And so it was for the first six months. Michael learned quickly, stayed energetic, and made friends with his coworkers. At his first performance review he was told he was a good example for the rest of the employees. Not long after, when a couple of assistant managers left, the general manager offered him a promotion to one of those vacancies. "I was thrilled,"

Michael said. "After only six months I was being offered a promotion, more money, and something that seemed to look pretty nice on a resume."

That feeling of excitement soon evaporated. On his first managing shift, everything seemed to be going pretty well until the general manager left the scene. "Then the revolution began," Michael told us.

> I began to ask my coworkers to do things. Simple things like taking in a laser tag game or restocking the snack counter. Only one of them would listen to me. . . . There was nothing I could do to make them work. It seemed no amount of threats, begging, or pleading would make them budge, so I told them to go home. . . . My one ally and I worked far after our shifts had ended to clean and prepare Ultrazone for the next day. I got home well after midnight.

"I hadn't earned my coworkers' trust and respect," Michael concluded. "I hadn't established my credibility." What could he do to earn their respect? "I decided that I had to determine what kind of manager I wanted to be, be clear about my values and then be true to them," he said. High on the list were his commitment to cooperation, collaboration, and camaraderie. "I decided I would never order my coworkers to do things, and I would be a good listener and stay completely open to any suggestions they might have."

In time his coworkers began to see that his behavior was a consistent reflection of Michael's new clarity about effective leadership.

> Within a few weeks, everyone was back on board. They had finally realized that I was a different sort of manager. Someone they wanted to work with . . . I asked people to do things, not commanded it. I wouldn't go sit in the office while everyone else cleaned at the end of the night. I would help them vacuum and

clean the bathrooms. . . . I never made demands, and I helped my coworkers even when it wasn't part of my job. By going above and beyond what my job required, I received more respect and found myself in a happier, more pleasant and productive workplace.

As Michael learned at Ultrazone, leaders can never take their credibility for granted, because *credibility is the foundation of leadership.* If people don't believe in the messenger, they won't believe the message. Leaders have to earn respect every day by staying true to their values and by acting on their beliefs. Leading by example is how leaders make visions and values tangible—how you demonstrate that you are personally committed. And because you're leading a group of people—not just leading yourself—modeling the way is also about what those who are following you are doing. How consistent are their words and deeds? How well are they practicing what's preached? As the leader, you're held accountable for their actions too.

CLARIFY VALUES

To do what you say, you have to know what you want to say. To earn and sustain personal credibility, you must be able to clearly articulate deeply held beliefs. That's why *clarifying values* leads the discussion of Model the Way. It's where it all begins.

Upon graduating from high school, Tammy Levy chose to move to Israel for a year. Many of her friends were going to be studying in American universities but, she told us, "I wanted to do something different and really immerse myself in the culture." After that year in Israel, she decided to stay and go to college there. She developed a passion for the country and was willing to leave her family and friends to pursue this passion.

> My two years in Israel forced me to think about myself as a person, my religious beliefs, my political beliefs, my actions, etc. It was a period of true introspection; a selfish time during which I struggled and fought within myself to find myself. . . . Moving back to America shook my world all over again but also provided me with an outlet to gain back much self confidence that I lost while in a foreign country and out of my element.

Tammy decided to take the classes and get involved in the extracurricular activities that interested her most. In the process, she found a passion for industrial organizational psychology. She worked on group projects that earned A's, and she completed independent study assignments that won high praise. She began working in the industrial organization graduate lab, became a full-fledged research assistant, and received grades that would make anyone proud. Most important, she said, "I became proud of what I do and who I've become."

> I recognize that throughout life I will continuously develop and learn. I will continue to introspect and question myself. I want to constantly question myself and question the thoughts and beliefs I decided upon only years before. Without this continuous inner fight I will not grow and will not learn. I recognize that there is always room for improvement and that I will never be perfect. But I also know that I am strong and confident and have a lot to offer. I work well with others and I work well as a leader.

Research shows that the people most frequently mentioned as admired leaders all had strong beliefs about matters of principle, an unwavering commitment to a clear set of values, and passion about their causes. The lesson is clear: the leaders who are admired most are those who believe strongly in something and are willing to stand up for their beliefs.

> *As long as one keeps searching, the answers come.*
>
> —Joan Baez

To stand up for your beliefs, you first have to know what they are. As Michael, Tammy, and other students found out, the learning comes from exploring yourself, your inner territory. This means you fully examine the values and assumptions that drive you, choose the principles you'll use to guide your actions, and become clear about the message you want to deliver. You then need to communicate your beliefs in ways that uniquely represent who you are; in other words, you need to be authentic.

You can be authentic only when you lead according to the principles that matter most to you. Otherwise you're just putting on an act. You will not have the integrity to lead. And if you do not "find your voice"—if the words you speak are not your own—you will not, in the long term, be able to be consistent in word and deed.

Kevin Koo found his voice as a leader of social change early in his college experience.

Growing up in rural New Hampshire as part of a small racial minority, I had encountered and endured prejudices from an early age. But one day during my freshman year, I witnessed these tensions escalate into violence. Four students, two white and two black, were engaged in a bloody fistfight while their peers on each side of the color line cheered them on. At that moment, I realized my safety and that of my peers could be irreversibly compromised. As officials armed with handcuffs and probations rushed in to end the fight, I could no longer accept such a short-term response; instead, I resolved to develop a long-term solution.

Kevin's solution was to organize a campus organization called Citizens of the World (C.O.W.) to "build bridges of awareness." He mobilized groups across campus to teach one another about their inherent diversity. "Harnessing this newfound understanding," Kevin told us, "we targeted prejudice by making racial slurs socially unpopular. I was amazed at how enthusiastically my peers embraced this initiative; not long after its introduction, I heard them responding to racial epithets with a firm 'Hey, not in our school!'"

In the context of Model the Way, values are defined as "enduring beliefs about *how* things should be accomplished." Your values supply a moral compass by which to navigate the course of your daily life. Values are most important in difficult times when daily challenges can easily throw you off course. Being clear about your values will give you the confidence to make the tough decisions, to act with determination, and to take charge of your life.

Though burdened with injuries throughout the season, runner Steve Hull still wanted to compete in the league finals in an event where, that particular year, there were three times as many runners as usual. "I just wanted to run my event," he told us, "but too many athletes and too many injuries prevented me from getting the chance to qualify for it." However, he added, "My mentor told me that circumstances do not have to dictate how I deal with life, or define who I am."

> So I did what I did best: practice. . . . I didn't miss a day. I ate right, I slept right, and I cheered for every runner competing in the spot I wanted. When the league finals came, I was not selected for my event. But since I was a senior, Coach put me in two other events to finish the season, which I did—dead last in each.

At the team banquet at the end of that season, after all the awards for MVPs and improved athletes, there would be one last award, the team's coach said. It would go to an athlete who was dedicated to having the best running form and always taking the sport very seriously. Steve told us,

> Then Coach mentioned how before league finals, several younger runners had come to him and asked that this particular runner take their place—he deserved it more than them. Coach said he had never had such an experience, where young men were stepping aside from glory for awe over one athlete's determination throughout an injury-laden season. This athlete never competed in his chosen event but showed by example how a true athlete conquers his challenges. And then Coach said, "This year's award for most Inspirational Athlete for the entire track and field team goes to Steve Hull!"

Steve had demonstrated to himself and others the importance of aligning his values with his actions. "The words Coach said were amazing," Steve told us. "And then I realized they were true."

> I learned I just don't know who is watching me. In the most insignificant moments, more talented athletes respected me whether I knew it or not. They saw how badly I wanted something by my actions. The award did not go to team captains or prize-winning runners, but to a true athlete. In leadership we cannot neglect the original roles we fill—before I was ever to reach my goal, I first had to be an athlete.

Values set the boundaries for your decisions—your commitments to personal and organizational goals—and they serve as guides to action. They help you be more in control of your life, and they motivate by keeping you focused on why you're doing what you're doing and the ends toward which you're striving.

> *Do not follow where the path may lead.*
>
> *Go instead where there is no path and leave a trail.*
>
> —Ralph Waldo Emerson

"The day I first picked up skateboarding was the day I knew I would take it very far," Jorge Chavez explained. "I didn't stop until I was the best at what I did." His determination, competitive spirit, and commitment to performing at the highest levels of achievement in his sport began to pay off. Over the next eight years, he picked up many sponsors, skated in competitions and demos, and starred in videos. And then one day, Jorge says, after watching a skate video, "I was struck with the idea of being part of a team, or a skate crew as some may call it." He rounded up a few skate friends and started a well-known crew, the YNII (You're Not in It) of Redwood City, California.

When they were first getting going, "I knew that my friends looked up to me," he told us. "I felt that by exceeding in the sport, I would be able to give back and encourage others to do their best as well. So I was moving forward and trying to model the way for them. Many of them struggled, but . . . we were all there for each other, and that is why we were a team, and not just a team but best friends."

The crew began attracting attention, gaining wider recognition, and picking up sponsors. Eventually YNII attained their goal: in Jorge's words, "to reach success and perhaps surpass me in the sport."

> I believe that in order to lead a group of people to success, you need to have reached that success yourself, and be able to pass it on. You must teach them everything you know and not hold anything back. . . . We all need to start somewhere, but with hard work and dedication, we can master what we do and surpass those who have taught us on the way.

As Jorge learned from personal experience, you must not only use your values to guide your actions, but also give voice to those values in ways that are uniquely your own, so people know that you are the one who's speaking.

One route to a true and genuine voice is to be more conscious about the way you communicate. Take it from Maya Babu, who as a college freshman was asked to serve as lead fellow of an initiative sponsored by her university to promote mentoring and after-school activities for youth in the metropolitan area. This new position required that she manage fourteen undergraduate and graduate fellows.

> One of the fourteen fellows I was to manage was a pediatrician completing a fellowship in adolescent health. This fellow was considerably older and more educated than I. Our relationship was strained from the beginning: I attempted in vain to contact him several times via email and phone. The rare responses he did send were usually notices that he would not attend mandatory fellow activities.
>
> I struggled with the situation; I could not understand why he was so unwilling to engage in group activities. Though I knew he was farther along in his career than I, I knew that I possessed greater expertise about this specific program. Only after conversing with several close mentors about the situation did I realize that his view of me, as an inexperienced young person, likely undermined his respect for my leadership abilities. Armed with this insight, I attacked the problem anew. I met with both the fellow and his immediate supervisor, described my experience and role with the program, and acknowledged several times my respect for the fellow's experience and work. Following these meetings, our communication improved.

Everything you say and do tells others how you view the world. You are free to choose what you want to express and the way you want to express it. In fact, you have a responsibility to your constituents to express yourself in an authentic manner—in a way they would immediately recognize as yours.

But student leaders aren't just speaking for themselves when they talk about the values that should guide decisions and actions. When leaders passionately express a commitment to some core value, they are not just saying, "I believe in this." They're making a commitment for an entire group. They're saying, "We all believe in this." Therefore, leaders must not only be clear about their own personal values but also make sure that there's agreement on a set of shared values among everyone they lead.

> *Leadership has a harder job to do than just choose sides. It must bring sides together.*
>
> —Jesse Jackson

For example, when Mark Micheli talks with potential new members for his fraternity, he not only tells them about the fraternity's cardinal principles but also explains why they were important to him in pledging the chapter at his university. He also uses these principles to make it clear how their chapter is different from other fraternities on campus and why the activities his chapter brothers are engaged in on campus reflect these principles. Says Mark, "We've all come to accept these principles as standards by which we want to live and run our fraternity."

SET THE EXAMPLE

Bradley Farr used his family's move from the Virgin Islands back to the United States as the inspiration to consciously decide that he was never again going to get into an argument with his parents. As the second oldest of four children, Bradley said, "I had seen plenty of arguing, growing up. And I had seen that it didn't get anybody anywhere and that things generally ended with hard feelings that took time to get over." Bradley felt that if he could accomplish that goal, it would set a good example for his younger brother and sister and significantly improve relationships within the family—and it did.

> If we disagreed about something . . . we talked it out like adults should do. It didn't mean that we were never frustrated or felt like we were misunderstood, it just meant that there was no reason to yell at each other and call each other names or do anything of the sort. I really feel that I set a good example in that regard and then my little sister and brother were able to see that it could be done, and slowly they stopped arguing so much with my parents.

Leaders practice what they preach—they are serious about their duty to represent their values and standards to the rest of the world, and to live up to them to the best of their abilities.

"I knew the importance of disciplined practice, so I consciously made an effort to set the right example during golf practices," golf team cocaptain Michael Haenel explained. During practice, he would pay extra attention to the details of "doing the right thing," like putting an aiming club down while hitting balls and devoting sufficient time and attention to the short game, chipping and putting.

> I knew the younger players and even my peers were looking up to me. . . . The underclassmen on the team and even the other seniors would see my serious dedication and it would rub off on them, inspiring them to practice with greater discipline. The team was able to develop solid practice habits and thus improve each one of their golf games.

Tan Jek Hau Benny was a camp commandant for a mountain-climbing expedition when he realized how important it is for leaders to set the example. He was working with sixty secondary school students climbing Mount Ophir in Malaysia as part of a leadership development program. "I was inevitably an often-seen figure to the students, even to those who were not attached to me in my sub-grouping," he told us.

From ensuring the safety of the group to facilitating small group discussions, he said, "I sought to constantly set myself as a role model in leadership and to do what I said I would do. . . ."

> I learned that one of the best ways to elicit a good effort from the entire team is for the leader to take the initiative and put his best effort into the task at hand. By setting a standard for the team to emulate, this would also ensure that the team remains a single cohesive and hardworking entity.

When they Model the Way, student leaders become role models for what the whole group (the team, the club, the chapter, the work group, the service organization) stands for. They also create a climate that makes it possible for everyone to align themselves with shared values.

> ***It's the frames which make some things important and some things forgotten. It's all only frames from which the content rises.***
>
> —Eve Babitz

One of the ways in which you can exemplify the shared values in your organization is to spend your time and attention wisely. Spend this precious nonrenewable resource on the most important values. For example, while cocaptain of his golf team, Michael Haenel didn't party during the season even though some of his friends did. "This behavior proved to my teammates that I was motivated to achieve a common goal," he said.

> This sense of motivation was contagious among the rest of the team and created a healthy team environment. Also, I would always show up to practice and team meetings on time. Both of these small actions had some big results for developing productive team chemistry. [Because of my] exemplifying motivation through my behavior, the team was able to unite and strive to do our best.

Signal-sending opportunities like these offer a chance to make visible and tangible to others your personal commitment to your group and its values. Simple though they may appear, each affords the chance to show where you stand on matters of principle. Exemplary leaders are very mindful of the signals they send and how they send them.

Will Jopling learned about "signal-sending" on a community service trip with his church group to work with Habitat for Humanity in Hungary. "My group was going to be digging trenches for the piping and foundation of an apartment building," he explained. "I didn't have much responsibility even though I was one of the oldest in the group. No matter where we were on the site, there was a supervisor monitoring our every move. . . ."

On their second day there it began to rain. Not only was it uncomfortable working in wet clothing, but they were also digging in mud the entire time. As it got wetter and wetter, Will said, the work grew extremely difficult because they had to watch out for mud sliding into the trench and ruining the foundation.

> You could see in every person's eyes that they were miserable and that the last thing they wanted to be doing was digging in the wet mud. Even I began to slow down . . . and that night, recollecting my thoughts on the day, I felt terrible about my effort.

To make matters worse, the next morning Will's group was told that they were way behind schedule. Because they had slacked off, the paid workers hired by Habitat for Humanity would have to make up for the group's lost time and bad work. "I looked at the people in my church group and saw that they didn't care at all," Will said. "I didn't want that to be me. . . . I told myself that I was here to work for poor Hungarian families and that if I did not work hard, it made it harder on those families. By working hard I would be able to feel good about making it easier for those families to have a home."

Will began the next day with a newly inspired commitment to make up for lost time. "Whenever someone needed help with anything I lent a hand," he told us. "I would do the grunt work that nobody else wanted to do. . . . Little did I know I was leading by example. It only took one person to recognize that I had the ability to lead."

On the following day, their last on the project, Will was asked to lead one of only two groups to work without a Habitat supervisor. "I was shocked to hear that the project supervisor wanted me to be in charge and trusted me with a serious job," Will said. Their assignment was to dig a deep narrow trench for an electrical pipe, put the piping in the trench, and cover the trench back up with dirt. Morale was still low because of the rainy days before—but, Will told us, "I looked past that and realized that we all could sit there and be miserable or actually get something done so we could all feel good about ourselves."

I gathered the team together and after I plunged my shovel into the mud we all began. The work was monotonous and tiresome but we kept going. When more and more people were going on longer and longer breaks I went and took just a few sips of water and then went right back. I was hoping that they would feel bad for not working that hard, and it paid off. In just a few moments the rest of my group was back working. . . . When I would start trying harder, they would follow suit and by the end of the day we had accomplished our goal.

On that muddy construction site in Hungary, Will realized what all exemplary student leaders know about Model the Way:

Leading by example was by far the most effective way for me to get the needed objectives accomplished. I did not overwhelm the people under me by talking and trying to encourage them. I acted and urged them by my actions to follow with me. Some people can deliver speeches to encourage people to do things, but the best way for a leader to inspire someone is to act.

> **Setting an example is not the main means of influencing others, it is the only means.**
> —Albert Einstein

Remember, too, that modeling the way is not just what you yourself do that demonstrates consistency between word and deed. Everyone else in your group—team member, partner, coworker, or colleague—also sends signals about what's valued, and they also set an example. Part of leadership is making sure that their actions are aligned with the shared values in your organization.

Remember Kevin Koo's experience with founding Citizens of the World? As the group developed on his campus, individual students—once isolated by their differences—joined together in support of social change. "Peer-to-peer education methods had empowered these young people, both as individuals and as a united front, to reject what they now recognized as unacceptable," he told us. "In this newly supportive social climate, minority students like me, once relegated to '*that* table' on the other side of the dining hall, were welcome to share the unique thoughts and experiences that transcended the color of our skin and the neighborhood in which we lived. In raising these issues of diversity on our campus, we established a platform from which to sustain permanent change."

So it's not just what leaders do that matters. Student leaders are also measured by how consistent their constituents' actions are with shared values, so leaders must teach others how to set an example.

REVIEW AND PRACTICE

The very first step on the journey to credible leadership is clarifying your values—discovering those fundamental beliefs that will guide your decisions and actions along the path to success and significance. Your personal values drive your commitment to be a credible leader. You can't do what you say if you don't know what you believe. And you can't do what you say if you don't believe in what you're saying.

Although personal values clarity is essential for all leaders, it's not enough. That's because student leaders don't just speak for themselves— they speak for their constituents as well. There must be agreement on the *shared values* that everyone will commit to upholding.

Student leaders demonstrate their intense commitment to the values they espouse by setting an example. It's how they earn and sustain credibility over time. Setting the example is all about execution and action. It's all about *doing* what you say. Student leaders who are seen as practicing what they preach are more effective than those leaders who don't.

One of the toughest parts about being a leader is that you're always onstage. People are always watching you, always talking about you. They're always testing your credibility. That's why setting the *right* example is so important and why it's essential to make use of all the tools you have available to you to Model the Way.

Here are some activities to help you get started to Model the Way.

I. DISCOVERING MY VALUES

Think back over the last few years and recall the projects, class assignments, clubs, teams, and programs you have been part of, whether you were the leader or not. Identify two or three that were most meaningful, energizing, enriching, and fun for you. What would you say characterized these experiences? What made you want to continue to be part of them? Make a list of these attributes:

1.

2.

3.

4.

5.

6.

7.

Now, take a look at the attributes you've listed and think about what they say about what you *value* in the activities you find most meaningful, energizing, enriching, and fun. For example, you might say, "One of the things I liked most was the chance to do things I had never done before." This might tell you that *challenge, innovation,* and *exploration* are important to you. Another way of examining the list of attributes is to ask yourself, "What values and actions are important to me in creating a climate in which I feel motivated, excited, and fulfilled?" Based on your observations and reflections, make a list of your underlying values.

1.

2.

3.

4.

5.

II. WHAT VALUES MATTER TO ME?

Listed here are more than seventy values. Look over this list and circle eight to ten of them that are most important to you. There are no wrong answers, and, if you don't find the right value in this list, then use the space provided to add the word(s) that best express your important values.

Achievement	Effectiveness
Autonomy	Empathy
Beauty	Equality
Caring	Fairness
Caution	Family
Challenge	Family time
Communication	Flexibility
Competence	Freedom
Competition	Friendship
Cooperation	Fun
Courage	Growth
Creativity	Happiness
Curiosity	Harmony
Customer focus	Health
Decisiveness	Honesty and integrity
Dependability	Hope
Determination	Human relationships
Discipline	Humor
Diversity	Independence

Individualism	Service to others
Innovation	Simplicity
Intelligence	Speed
Involvement	Spirituality and faith
Learning	Strength
Love and affection	Success
Loyalty	Task focus
Open-mindedness	Teamwork
Organization	Trust
Patience	Truth
Power	Uniqueness
Productivity	Variety
Profitability	Winning
Prosperity and wealth	Wisdom
Quality	_____
Quantity	_____
Recognition	_____
Respect	_____
Responsibility	_____
Risk-taking	_____
Security	_____

Take a look at the values you circled or added. Now select the *five* that are most important to you and write them in the following space. If you can, rank them in order of importance, with #1 being your most important value. Next to each value, write a statement about why you selected this value.

Value   **This is important to me because:**

1.

2.

Value	This is important to me because:

3.

4.

5.

With one or more of your classmates, share your list of key values and why they are important to you.

III. PUTTING MY VALUES INTO PRACTICE

Leaders don't just "talk the talk" when it comes to values; they "*walk the talk.*" So how have you put your values into practice? Select a value that is important to you and write a brief scenario describing an action you took that demonstrated that this value was important to you. For instance, if "service to others" is important to you, you might write about a time when you volunteered to serve dinner at the local shelter on Thanksgiving or about the time when you joined a group of friends and headed down to Louisiana to help rebuild the community after Hurricane Katrina. In other words, where's the evidence that you *walk your talk*?

FURTHER REFLECTIONS

- Before you accept or take on a new assignment or responsibility, find ways to ask about the values that will guide decisions and actions. Make sure there is a good fit between your personal values and those required in this assignment.

- Before you ask others to take on a new assignment or responsibility, answer the question: "Why should anyone follow me?" Be sure you communicate with others on your team and in your organization about who you are as a person and what you value in others and in relationships.

- Keep track of how you spend your time. Check to see whether your actions are consistent with your values and with what you and others have agreed is important. If you find inconsistencies, figure out what you need to do to align your actions with those values. Alternatively, be honest with yourself and stop calling these your values if they don't line up with your actions.

- Admit your mistakes. Say, "I don't know." Show that you're willing to change your mind when someone comes up with a better idea.

INSPIRE A
SHARED VISION

Jen Marsh had volunteered for a special program to help children learn how to read. She says that on the first day she arrived,

> I took my seat in a miniature chair, and a little boy came up to me and asked, "Why are you wasting your summer here?" At first I was surprised by the question, but then I realized that he just wanted to see if I was going to stay. I replied by telling him how I genuinely wanted to be there and that I would be his reading buddy for the day. With this remark his eyes got bigger, and he even let out a tiny smile.

Not long after, Jen discovered a leadership insight: "There was no way I was going to get these second and third graders to read because *I* wanted them to; instead it was something that I had to help them want to accomplish on their own. I had to get the kids excited about reading and show them how important this achievement would be later on in their lives."

All the children saw reading as a difficult chore, and they would try to avoid it as much as possible. "Originally I got frustrated with the kids and they got on my nerves," Jen told us, "but I soon realized that it would take time for my vision to become our vision. I needed to better understand the minds of the children, and this could only be perfected by seeing eye-to-eye with them."

Jen says she will never forget her excitement when she witnessed the young child she had met on the first day finish an entire book all by himself. "When he looked into my eyes and saw how happy I was for him, it finally clicked in him why I had come to volunteer in his school," she explained.

He could instantly perceive how proud I was, and in return he extended his learning to his classmates. After we had come together in our common vision, leadership was put into the hands of the students. During the beginning of the week the kids would always pick out the shortest stories with several pictures to read, but by the end of the week they were trying to show off to me and the other kids that they could read the harder books. When the students came across a new word they would seek help from their peers and slowly sound it out all by themselves. Collectively we had turned a once impossible chore into a new and enjoyable activity.

When Jen realized that she needed to "see eye-to-eye" with those children, she gained an insight all exemplary student leaders share: Vision comes from relationships with others. You are much more likely to step forward when you feel passionate about the legacy you want to leave and about the kind of world you want for others. Leadership is not simply about what you want for yourself; it's also about what others want for themselves. Exemplary leaders understand the hopes and dreams of their constituents, and they are able to forge a unity of common aspirations. It's this collective understanding of a mutually desirable future that inspires people to share a common vision of the future.

Exemplary student leaders are able to *envision the future,* to gaze across the horizon of time and imagine the greater opportunities to come. They imagine that extraordinary feats are possible and that the ordinary could be transformed into something noble. They are able to develop an ideal and unique image of the future for the common good.

So it's not just the leader's vision that matters. It's the shared vision. Everyone has dreams and aspirations. We all think about the future; we all want tomorrow to be better than today. Student leaders have to make sure that what they see is also something that others can see. When visions are shared they attract more people, sustain higher levels of motivation, and withstand more challenges than those that are yours alone.

ENVISION THE FUTURE

As Jen showed with those second and third graders learning how to read, student leaders are possibility thinkers. All enterprises, big or small, begin with imagination and the belief that what's merely an image today can be made real in the future. Turning possibility thinking into a clear shared vision is the leader's challenge—especially through the difficult times, when things seem to be changing at warp speed.

Look at it this way. Imagine you're driving along the Pacific Coast Highway, heading south from San Francisco on a bright, sunny day. The hills are on your left; the ocean, on your right. On some curves, the cliffs plunge several hundred feet to the water. You can see for miles and miles. You're cruising along at the speed limit, music blaring, top down, wind in your hair, and not a care in the world. Suddenly, without warning, you come around a bend in the road and there's a blanket of fog as thick as you've ever seen. What do you do?

We've asked this question many, many times, and we get the same answers:

- I slow way down.
- I turn my lights on.
- I grab the steering wheel with both hands.
- I tense up.
- I sit up straight or lean forward.
- I turn the music off so I can hear better.

Then you go around the next curve in the road, the fog lifts, and it's clear again. What do you do? You relax, speed up, turn the lights off, put the music back on, and enjoy the scenery.

This analogy illustrates the importance of clarity of vision, especially when you're going fast. Are you able to go faster when it's foggy or when it's clear? How fast can you drive in the fog without risking your own or other people's lives? How comfortable are you riding in a car with someone else who drives fast in the fog? The answers are obvious, aren't they?

You're better able to go fast when your vision is clear. You're better able to anticipate the switchbacks and bumps in the road when you can see ahead. There are always going to be times when the sun hides behind the clouds or the fog makes it difficult to maneuver, but when it comes to traveling fast it's definitely preferable to be able to see farther ahead.

The point is simply this: To become a leader you must be able to envision the future. The speed of change doesn't alter this fundamental truth about leadership. People only want to follow those who can see beyond today's problems and clearly visualize a brighter tomorrow.

We know not where our dreams will take us,

but we can probably see quite clearly

where we'll go without them.

—Marilyn Grey

Clarifying your vision, like clarifying your values, is an intuitive, emotional process. There's often no logic to it. Visions are reflections of your fundamental beliefs and assumptions about the world: human nature, technology, economics, science, politics, art, and ethics. Much like a literary or musical theme, your vision is the broad message that you want to convey, the primary melody that you want people to remember.

Envisioning the future begins with passion, feeling, concern, or an inspiration that something is worth doing. The vision gets clearer as you act, pay attention, experience, and immerse yourself in it, until you can articulate it for your constituents.

Alyssa Giagliani ran track and cross-country on the varsity team in her freshman year and remembers talking with the freshman team at the end of their first season. They had won the freshman division title race, and Alyssa asked them what they saw in their team's future. They said they didn't think they had a future in running.

The freshmen then asked Alyssa the same question right back, and she told them, "I see a great potential: the potential to be the first women's team in the history of our school to make the championships, win league titles and a division title." She told us that these goals had never crossed their minds. "I could see that the freshmen, my future teammates, were enlightened by this idea and that they were willing to put in hard work in order to attain those lofty goals."

In her senior year, Alyssa was in a terrible auto accident, with life-threatening injuries including a broken back, collapsed lung, and multiple leg fractures. The doctors thought that she would be lucky to simply survive the night. Obviously her track and cross-country days were over. Her teammates said they didn't have the heart to finish the season without her. When Alyssa heard this she was flabbergasted: "We were now in the championship phase of the season, we had only one month left, and they wanted to quit! I knew that I had to inspire them somehow."

Lying in her hospital bed, she made no bones about her disagreement with her teammates about their quitting. "I expressed my beliefs forcefully," she said. "I made a deal with my team that if they finished the season I would be walking with them to the starting line the day of the race. . . . This way of getting my point across made my teammates realize that I was passionate about them finishing what they started."

> As the race day was approaching I tried my best to excite the team and rally some enthusiasm even though I was disappointed I couldn't take part in the race. My enthusiasm and support spread through the entire team and they seemed solely focused on their goal. The look on each and every one of their faces before the race embodied a passion for success. My positive attitude helped them cross the finish line that day. My teammates realized how far they came in the course of one year and were inspired to run straight towards their goal. We became the first women's cross-country team in the history of our school to advance to the championship meet and the first team to win a major title.

Student leaders like Alyssa want to do something significant—to accomplish something no one else has yet achieved—and that sense of meaning and purpose must come from within. Research shows that people who are self-motivated keep working toward a result even if there's no reward for them personally, whereas people who are externally controlled are likely to stop trying when rewards or punishments are removed.

Everyone has concerns, desires, questions, propositions, agendas, aspirations, hopes, and dreams. Whatever you call them, these are the things that are much more important to us than others. You need to be able to name it for yourself so that you can talk about it with others.

Consider the journey taken by William Hwang, who founded United InnoWorks Academy, a non-profit dedicated to opening the world of science, engineering, and medicine to underprivileged children and igniting their love for learning. His passion was ignited in high school, when William was one of 400 magnet-program students attending a socioeconomically disadvantaged school of 3,200 students. "Incarcerated fathers, single mothers, and poor role models suddenly jumped from the evening news to cold reality," he told us.

> Through sports, I befriended many local students, including my sprinting partner, Tony. He was hard-working and smart, so imagine my shock when he once told me he had to go meet his parole officer after practice. . . . Through his eyes, I discovered the unseen hardships and lack of opportunities underprivileged kids face. Just as intelligent and diligent, their futures were bleak, unable to relate school learning with their realities. When I missed practice for academic competitions, Tony always took a reserved interest in this "other world." He deserved better opportunities and I know part of him wished his life were different. When I fulfilled my promise to contact him after graduation, the slamming of the phone after a brusque "He doesn't live here anymore" saddened me, but since that day, my friend Tony has not strayed far from my mind.

William's friendship with Tony enabled him to articulate an exciting and ennobling possibility for InnoWorks: "Although we are students, we *can* change the world as leaders and volunteers. There is no reason to wait until we are established and settled."

Education is the future and I believe all children deserve access to high-quality educational opportunities. Extracurricular educational programs have changed, reshaped, and motivated me in amazing ways, helping me focus and see new and exciting possibilities. These programs are often out of reach for the underserved children that need them most. I wanted to change that and help them overcome their obstacles and share my passion for learning. I may be too late for some of my friends, but I can be there for all the children who continue to lack the chances they did.

Beginning with a single program in 2003, InnoWorks has nurtured more than five hundred students at eight university chapters around the world and continues to grow rapidly. The organization was selected by CNN for a 2007 BR!CK Award, the "Oscar of youth service."

> *You don't lead by pointing and telling*
> *people some place to go. You lead by going*
> *to that place and making a case.*
>
> —Ken Kesey

As important as your own passion and commitment are to envisioning exciting possibilities for the future, it's important to realize that leaders can't impose their vision on others—the vision must have meaning to their constituents as well. What other students really want to hear about is *their own* aspirations. They want to hear how *their* dreams will come true and *their* hopes will be fulfilled. They want to see themselves in the picture of the future that the leader is painting. The very best student leaders understand that their key task is inspiring a *shared* vision, not selling their own view of the world.

Take it from Kevin Koo, who began telling us his story in Chapter Three about founding Citizens of the World (C.O.W.) in response to racial tensions at his college. "In raising issues of diversity, I simply established a platform, which was then guided and adopted by my peers, from which to sustain permanent change." From an initial peer-to-peer education program, C.O.W. flourished as individual students, once isolated by their differences, joined together to "build bridges of awareness." As Kevin tells it,

> C.O.W. emerged not only as an organization committed to building bridges of understanding and supporting the minority voice, but also as a springboard for positive action. One student's idea to share her artistic heritage blossomed into an annual, community-wide celebration attracting 10,000 participants. A C.O.W.-sponsored media acquisition initiative benefiting resource-poor schools developed into a global literacy campaign. And with the support of the local community, C.O.W. was the impetus behind changes in school policy that have reduced violence and crime twofold. By reaching out to at-risk youth, engaging rival cliques in productive discussion, and promoting service-learning as a means of conflict resolution, C.O.W. has become a model emulated on other campuses, as well as a testament to the power of youth inspired by the promise of a better tomorrow.

As Kevin and his constituents made clear, leaders must show others how they, too, will be served by the long-term vision of the future and demonstrate how their specific needs can be satisfied. By knowing their constituents, listening to them, and finding out what's meaningful to them, leaders are able to give voice to constituents' feelings and make their shared vision a cause for commitment.

When students are part of something that's important to them they develop a sense of belonging to something very special. This sense of belonging is key to gaining commitment—something that's especially important when the going gets tough.

ENLIST OTHERS

Student leaders begin with the assumption that anything is possible; it's this belief that gets them through difficult times. The leader's challenge is to turn that assumption into an inspiring, shared vision—*an ideal and unique image of the future for the common good.*

Vast reserves of energy and excitement are needed to sustain commitment to a distant dream, and as a leader you are expected to be a major source of that energy. Leaders know that in order to get extraordinary things done everyone has to fervently believe in and commit to a common purpose.

Exemplary student leaders also know that leadership is a dialogue, not a monologue. Conversations about people's lives, hopes, and dreams are required to develop a shared sense of purpose. Leaders help other students see that what they are doing is bigger than themselves, something that lifts their moral and motivational levels. That's what we mean when we say that leaders have to *enlist others.*

Yearbook editor Sheri Lee was enlisting others when she explained to the staff why she enjoyed working on the annual so much, despite the hard work:

> We are making something that will be treasured for the rest of our lives. *We* are in charge of preserving all the memories that occur during this school year and it is up to us to make sure that there is a yearbook to hand out at the end of the year. Just think, every time that you look at this year's yearbook, you can see that all your

hard work paid off in the pages that you created. When you are an alum, you can look back . . . and be proud that you were responsible for creating something so unique.

What truly pulls students forward, especially in difficult times, is the exciting possibility that what they are doing can make a difference to the future of their families, friends, colleagues, campuses and communities. They want to know that what they do matters.

> **The greatest danger for most of us is not**
> **that our aim is too high and we miss it,**
> **but that it is too low and we reach it.**
>
> —-Michelangelo

Exemplary student leaders also communicate what makes their group or organization—and its product or service—*unique.* Compelling visions set us apart from everyone else. Visions must differentiate us from others if we're to attract and retain volunteers, teammates, customers, donors, or supporters. That's exactly what David Chan Tar Wei and his committee did.

As David explained, they were working on inaugurating a new system of five "houses" intended to engender the competition and collaboration that would lead to greater school spirit and add more diversity to school life and culture.

We constantly reminded ourselves to be creative and explore revolutionary ideas that perhaps have never been thought of before. The houses did not have emblems that could represent them and hence, we felt strongly that house shirts and house crests could be used and accepted as formal symbols of identification. And . . . we sought to include aspects of the house into almost every school event, ranging from Teachers' Day to Open House to Orientation so as to create the house vibrancy and culture that we sought. . . . And this tied in with our vision to look after the welfare of the school population and represented our desire to have greater house collaboration and unity.

When students in your group or organization understand how they're truly distinctive and how they stand out in the crowd, they're a lot more eager to voluntarily sign up and invest their energies. Uniqueness also makes it possible for smaller groups within large organizations to have their own visions within the collective vision. Each can differentiate itself by finding its most distinctive qualities. Each can be proud of its ideal and unique image of its future as it works toward the common future of the larger organization.

> *One of the hardest things in life is having words in your heart that you can't utter.*
>
> —James Earl Jones

One of the most effective things student leaders can do to enlist others in a shared vision is to "animate" it. They are able to portray the vision so that others can see it, hear it, taste it, touch it, feel it. They use the power of symbolic language, a positive communication style, and nonverbal expressiveness to make the intangible tangible, breathing life into their visions. They use metaphors and other figures of speech; give examples, tell stories, and relate anecdotes; draw word pictures; and use quotations and slogans.

There is no better place to look for an example than to a master of this art: Dr. Martin Luther King Jr. His "I Have a Dream" speech tops the list of the best American public addresses of the twentieth century.

On August 28, 1963, on the steps of the Lincoln Memorial in Washington, D.C., before a throng of 250,000, King proclaimed his dream to the world. As he spoke, and as thousands clapped and shouted, a nation was moved.

As you read this text, imagine that you're there in the audience on that August day, listening to King. Imagine that you're there to better understand how King is so capable of moving people. Pay attention not just to the content but King's well-known delivery of these words and phrases. Think about the rhythm, the cadence, and the pauses. Place yourself on the steps of the Lincoln Memorial and feel how the audience reacted as they listened to these words:

> I say to you today, my friends, so even though we face the difficulties of today and tomorrow, I still have a dream. It is a dream deeply rooted in the American dream.
>
> I have a dream that one day this nation will rise up and live out the true meaning of its creed: "We hold these truths to be self-evident: that all men are created equal."
>
> I have a dream that one day on the red hills of Georgia the sons of former slaves and the sons of former slave owners will be able to sit down together at the table of brotherhood.
>
> I have a dream that one day even the state of Mississippi, a state sweltering with the heat of injustice, sweltering with the heat of oppression, will be transformed into an oasis of freedom and justice.
>
> I have a dream that my four little children will one day live in a nation where they will not be judged by the color of their skin but by the content of their character.
>
> I have a dream today.
>
> I have a dream that one day, down in Alabama, with its vicious racists, with its governor having his lips dripping with the words

of interposition and nullification, one day right there in Alabama, little black boys and black girls will be able to join hands with little white boys and white girls as sisters and brothers.

I have a dream today.

I have a dream that one day every valley shall be exalted, every hill and mountain shall be made low, the rough places will be made plains, and the crooked places will be made straight, and the glory of the Lord shall be revealed, and all flesh shall see it together.

This is our hope. This is the faith that I go back to the South with.

With this faith we will be able to transform the jangling discords of our nation into a beautiful symphony of brotherhood. With this faith we will be able to work together, to pray together, to struggle together, to go to jail together, to stand up for freedom together, knowing that we will be free one day.

This will be the day, this will be the day when all of God's children will be able to sing with a new meaning, "My country, 'tis of thee, sweet land of liberty, of thee I sing. Land where my fathers died, land of the pilgrim's pride, from every mountainside, let freedom ring."

And if America is to be a great nation this must become true.

So let freedom ring from the prodigious hilltops of New Hampshire.

Let freedom ring from the mighty mountains of New York.

Let freedom ring from the heightening Alleghenies of Pennsylvania!

Let freedom ring from the snowcapped Rockies of Colorado!

Let freedom ring from the curvaceous slopes of California!

But not only that; let freedom ring from Stone Mountain of Georgia!

Let freedom ring from Lookout Mountain of Tennessee!

Let freedom ring from every hill and molehill of Mississippi.

From every mountainside, let freedom ring.

And when this happens, and when we allow freedom ring, when we let it ring from every village and every hamlet, from every state and every city, we will be able to speed up that day when all of God's children, black men and white men, Jews and Gentiles, Protestants and Catholics, will be able to join hands and sing in the words of the old Negro spiritual, "Free at last! Free at last! Thank God Almighty, we are free at last!"

To enlist others, as King demonstrated, you have to help them *see* and *feel* how their own interests and aspirations are aligned with the vision. You have to paint a compelling picture of the future, one that enables constituents to experience viscerally what it would be like to actually experience and participate in an exciting and uplifting future. That's the only way they'll become internally motivated to commit their individual energies to its realization.

> **If you want to build a ship, don't herd people together to collect wood and don't assign them tasks and work, but rather teach them to long for the endless immensity of the sea.**
>
> ——Antoine de Saint-Exupery

"But I'm not like Dr. King," you say. "I can't possibly do what he did. Besides, he was a preacher, and I'm just a regular person." Most people initially respond this way. Of The Five Exemplary Student Leadership Practices, Inspire a Shared Vision is the one with which many students feel most uncomfortable, as they rarely consider themselves *inspiring*.

Even so, students nearly always become emotionally expressive when talking about their visions of the future. Listen to Alyssa Lee describe her experience after she stepped up as a freshman to serve as captain of a tennis team at her school that nobody thought had a future:

> Leadership found me out on that tennis court my freshman year. I might have been the first one to step up and take on the responsibilities as a leader, but by the end of the season, every one of those women on that team had become a leader in their own right as well. By having one shared vision, one common goal, we were able to accomplish goals that stand, to this day, as record breaking.
>
> There is no better feeling than to have somebody say they believe in you and believe in what you can do. Inspiring a shared vision is about just that. It's saying you and I both have a goal, I know we can do it together. That is something I will always take with me in any leadership experience I encounter for the rest of my life.

The assumption that the process of inspiring a shared vision is somehow mystical or supernatural inhibits people, making them feel that they have to be something special to be inspiring. But all that's really necessary is appealing to common ideals and developing the skills for communicating the shared vision with commitment and enthusiasm—just as Alyssa did with her tennis team, just as Martin Luther King did on the steps of the Lincoln Memorial.

You attract students to engage with and join you in a cause when you demonstrate an enthusiastic and genuine belief in the capacity of others; when you strengthen people's will, supply the means to achieve, and express optimism for the future. Constituents want student leaders who remain passionate despite obstacles and setbacks. In today's uncertain times, constituents want leaders with a can-do attitude, who make other students feel good about themselves and what they are doing.

The most admired student leaders are vigorous, active, and full of life, with a positive attitude and communication style. Some people call it charisma, but we have observed that people who are perceived to be charismatic are simply more animated than others—they smile more, speak faster, pronounce words more clearly, move their heads and bodies more often, and are more likely to make physical contact with others during greetings. What is referred to as charisma, then, can better be understood as energy and expressiveness. The old truism that enthusiasm is infectious is certainly true for student leaders. You do have to show your excitement if you expect others to get excited.

Emotion drives expressiveness; this means it's important to communicate your emotions using all the means of expression available to you—verbal and nonverbal—if you want to generate the intense enthusiasm that's required to mobilize people to make shared aspirations a reality. Emotion also makes things more memorable, so if you want your messages to be remembered, add more emotion to your words and behavior.

> **Those who hear not the music think the dancers mad.**
>
> —Chinese proverb

None of these suggestions will be of any value if you don't believe in what you're saying. *The prerequisite to enlisting others in a shared vision is genuineness.* The first place to look before talking to others about the vision of the future is in your heart.

REVIEW AND PRACTICE

The most important role of visions in organizational life is to give focus to human energy. To enable everyone concerned with an enterprise to see more clearly what's ahead of them, student leaders must have and convey an exciting and ennobling vision of the future. The path to clarity of visions comes from passion, from what people care about most deeply. Leaders can't effectively and authentically lead others to places they personally don't want to go.

Although you have to be clear about your own visions before you can expect other students to follow you, keep in mind that it's not one person's vision that people will willingly follow. If the vision is to be attractive to more than an insignificant few, it must appeal to all who have a stake in it. Only *shared* visions have the magnetic power to sustain commitment over time. Whether you're leading a three-person committee, a small community service project, a sports team, or an entire student body, a shared vision sets the agenda and gives direction and purpose to the enterprise. The process begins and ends with listening. Listening to the voices of all your constituents. Listening for their hopes, dreams, and aspirations.

Student leaders appeal to common ideals. They connect others to what is most meaningful in the shared vision. They lift people to higher levels of motivation and morality, and they continuously reinforce the fact that they can make a difference in the world. Exemplary student leaders speak to what is unique and singular about their group, making other students feel proud to be a part of something extraordinary. And the best leaders understand that it's not their personal idiosyncratic view of the future that's important; it's the aspirations of all their constituents that matter most.

Leaders must be able to breathe life into visions; they must animate them so that others can experience what it would be like to live and work in that ideal and unique future—whether it's a championship cross-country season or helping hurricane survivors rebuild their neighborhood. They use a variety of modes of expression to make their abstract visions concrete. Through skillful use of metaphors, symbols, word pictures, positive language, and personal energy, student leaders generate enthusiasm and excitement for the common vision. But above all, you must be convinced of the value of the shared vision and share that genuine belief with others. You must believe in what you are saying. Authenticity is the true test of conviction, and constituents will follow willingly only if they sense that the vision is genuine.

Here are some steps to take to develop your skills to Inspire a Shared Vision.

I. MY PAST AS PROLOGUE TO MY FUTURE

There are many synonyms for the idea of *vision,* but a key notion is being able to express your view of the future and how things could be uniquely and ideally better than they are today. One way to get started on your way to the future is to explore your past and in so doing identify key patterns and themes in your life choices.

Make a list of four or five experiences from your past that have been turning points for you. These are experiences that have truly influenced the direction you have taken in your life. Describe each experience in a few words:

1.

2.

3.

4.

5.

Now review the experiences in your list. Do you see a pattern? Is there a theme or two that connects them? Name the pattern and/or theme:

What do these patterns and themes from your life thus far tell you about what creates meaning for you? What does this tell you about your hopes and dreams for the future? What is likely to propel you forward?

II. IMAGINE THE POSSIBILITIES

Identify one project, activity, assignment, or event you are currently involved in:

What are your personal goals for this project or activity? In other words, what end goal do you want to achieve?

In what ways is this end goal (vision) important to what others want to achieve? Some may be the same as yours, but some may be different. What steps can be taken to find common ground so that others will share the vision and so they would want to work hard for this vision even if you weren't around?

When this project, activity, assignment, or event is over, what would you like to hear other people saying about it? How do these comments align with your vision?

III. GIVE LIFE TO YOUR VISION

You give life to a vision when you infuse it with powerful language, with metaphors, stories, word pictures, illustrations, and examples. Think of your vision as a song. Most songs are about the theme of *love.* But it would be pretty hard to sell a song that just repeated that one word over and over again. All songs are variations on a theme, and the ones that are remembered have a unique way of expressing their theme (even love!). Your vision needs to do the same.

Picture yourself, your team, and your organization at the end of the project, program, assignment, or activity. It has been successful beyond your wildest dreams. What do you see in this case? Describe it in rich detail by responding to these questions:

- What are people *doing*?

- What are people *saying*?

- How are people *feeling*?

The most powerful visions use a metaphor (a figure of speech that suggest a likeness between your project and something else) or visual analogy to change abstract ideas into tangible and meaningful images. For example, a skyscraper as a metaphor for a project can be used to illustrate and highlight many possible themes, like "reaching to the sky" or "requires lots of coordinated teamwork and a strong foundation" or "brings together a multitude of talents."

Take a few moments to identify a concrete object or activity that could serve as a metaphor for your own project, one that might be inspiring if your teammates hold it in their mind. For example, you could say your project is like a marathon, or the ascent of Mt. Everest, or an eagle's flight, or a revolution, or a skateboard. Try this yourself. Take three minutes to brainstorm and record a list of as many metaphors as you can.

My project is like:

From your list, select the metaphor that works best for you and your project. Explain how your project is like your metaphorical expression.

Metaphor	How It's Like This Project

FURTHER REFLECTIONS

- Speak positively. Don't say *try,* say *will.* Don't say *if,* say *when.* Sure, there are lots of reasons why this or that might not happen, and of course it will be hard work, but people don't get charged up when you are tentative and noncommittal.

- Get to know the people you are working with. Make a list of all the individuals or groups of individuals you want to enlist in your vision of the future. Think about not only all those who have a stake today but also those who will have a stake tomorrow in the outcomes of what you envision. Talk with them about their aspirations, hopes, and dreams.

- Don't be afraid to be repetitive. In real estate it's *location, location, location;* for leaders it is always *communicate, communicate, communicate.* Whatever it is that you want to accomplish, you must be willing to talk about it and why it is important, over and over again. Doing so also conveys your own personal commitment.

- Improve your presentation skills while in school. Take a public speaking class. Whenever possible, volunteer to stand in front of a group and speak, even if it's just to introduce someone or make an announcement. Spend a little time studying advertising and the performing arts. Both fields are rich sources of creative ideas on how to convey abstract concepts and how to appeal to human emotions.

5

CHALLENGE
THE PROCESS

"After hours of resume preparation, phone calls, interviews, and applications, I was finally hired as a hostess at a high-volume, deli-style restaurant in Seattle," Hannah Perlman recalled as she reflected on one of her personal-best leadership experiences.

> Relieved to finally have a job and a source of cash flow, I was not too concerned about the work itself. I did what I was supposed to; I greeted my customers with a smile, sat them down, and did any other little task my managers asked of me—nothing more, nothing less. At that point I was a lot more interested in chatting it up with my oh-so-cool twenty-something coworkers.

It was a large and busy restaurant, so Hannah had been instructed to follow management's seating chart and rotation, which allotted each server a certain number of tables assigned in a certain order. "As far as I was concerned," she said, "the system was working and there was no need for improvement."

Then one evening, during the "dreaded dinner hour rush," Hannah told us, "my social hour was suddenly compromised."

I observed the servers walking in and out of the kitchen and I noticed that some of them appeared quite stressed. Their pace was hurried and sweat beads were beginning to form on their foreheads. I would try and ease their minds by chatting and making jokes but I could sense that they were not in the mood. At the same time I also observed that other servers looked very at ease, almost bored. I looked down at my chart, reassuring myself that I had followed the seating rotation correctly. If I was doing everything according to plan, then why were the servers stressed out and, more importantly, why were customers coming up to me and asking why they had been sitting at their table for twenty minutes and they did not even have their sodas? At that moment I realized that despite the fact that I was doing everything *correctly,* it was still not *right.*

Hannah suddenly understood the problem: it was supposed to be an egalitarian system but, she said, "it was simply too equal." It was designed so the servers would have roughly the same number of tables, with table assignments spaced out over reasonable time intervals. But some of the servers had several years of experience and others were fresh out of high school, working in their first restaurant job.

"Though rotation is a good foundation," Hannah observed, "I realized that the servers also needed to be assigned according to their skill level. If they are strong, then give them a lot of tables at once, and conversely, if they're still learning, they need to be given fewer tables until they get stronger.

> Initially, I made my changes subtly. . . . Everyone looked as busy as everyone else and I had not received any complaints. The rules of the seating chart were bent, but certainly not broken. My little plan was going quite smoothly until my manager saw what I was doing. . . .
>
> The dreaded moment finally came when he asked me to come into his office to discuss my actions. He cut straight to the chase and said I went against company policy. . . . I explained that I took those particular actions because I was trying to make life easier for all the servers, but not undermine the higher authority. He still looked at me with displeasure. I then went on to say that over the course of these first few weeks at the restaurant I had noticed that there was a lot of variation between the servers' experience and skill levels and that some of them were too overwhelmed with their customers. This discourse went on for a few minutes and I was starting to get pretty frustrated. I finally took the high road and apologized for not consulting him. . . . I still got written up for going against company policy but he agreed that when the restaurant got busy that I could make a few exceptions to the rules. . . . I was also granted permission to give these instructions to my future trainees over the course of the summer.

What Hannah did at that restaurant is what all exemplary student leaders do: they willingly challenge the system to get new products, services, and systems adopted. "I realized that in any situation one can create rules and systems," Hannah told us in summing up her experience, "but behind all systems are real people—people who have different strengths and weaknesses. By simply recognizing my coworkers' strengths and weaknesses I was inspired to challenge the system and initiate some positive change."

SEARCH FOR OPPORTUNITIES

Personal-best leadership experiences always involve some sort of challenge. They are about radical departures from the past, about doing things that have never been done before, and about going to places not yet discovered. *The work of leaders is change.* And all change requires that leaders actively seek ways to make things better.

"My team was initially rather unconfident of being able to buck the trend and make Friendship Week a lot bigger than what it traditionally was," Amanda Zain said in explaining how she and her committee turned a lackluster annual function into "a spectacular event that would succeed in bringing the college together during this special week."

"In the early stages of planning there were suggestions to revert back to the tried and tested way of organizing the event because of the many hurdles we faced," she told us. Slowly but surely they forged ahead to create a new program to accommodate larger crowds and to move the main event—the Talent Time Finale—into the canteen where students congregated during their free time. They designed an outstanding publicity campaign to drum up interest and executed the whole event "in a first-of-its-kind way," Amanda said. "The week's events turned out to be a huge success . . . [and] we set a precedent for even bigger and better Friendship Weeks in the future."

Whether the impetus for change comes from outside challenges or from within yourself or your group, student leaders make things happen—they seize the initiative. And to make *new* things happen they actively seek innovative ideas from outside the boundaries of familiar experience.

Students describe their personal-best leadership experiences as *challenging, rewarding,* and *exciting*—humdrum situations just aren't associated with high-level performance. Leaders seize the initiative with enthusiasm, determination, and a desire to make something happen.

> *Not everything that is faced can be changed.*
>
> *But nothing can be changed until it is faced.*
>
> —James Baldwin

They are energized by the challenges of a difficult experience. "The sky is truly the limit," Junghans Tasani says he learned from his experience being on his college's student council. "Having had to balance my academic work with council work and being a first team member of the squash team . . . I realized that with sheer determination, it is possible to overcome all setbacks and meet seemingly impossible deadlines."

Research shows that leadership is inextricably connected to the process of innovation, which means changing the status quo. Student leaders must be innovators to improve the organization and keep it competitive. They must also be proactive, able to make something happen under conditions of extreme uncertainty and urgency—when leadership is most needed. Proactive people tend to work harder at what they do and persist at achieving their goals.

Regan Bergmark is a good example. When she transferred to another university in her sophomore year, she brought with her a commitment to form a new chapter of the Student Campaign for Child Survival (SCCS), an international children's health advocacy organization that seeks to improve children's health worldwide by increasing U.S. government funding for child survival programs. SCCS members meet with their legislative representatives, educate fellow students on global health issues, write op-eds and letters, and participate in hands-on "global-local" projects.

"Despite [the fact] that I had helped to organize SCCS national conferences, lobby days in Washington, D.C., and numerous campus events, starting a chapter at a new school on my own was daunting," Regan told us.

I needed to find students who were interested in joining the campaign and empower them to do high-quality advocacy work. On an administrative level, I needed to get the group registered, find a place to meet, set up email lists, and numerous other unglamorous tasks that are part of starting a movement on your campus.

Regan had just recruited her boyfriend (and now husband) Brian Bergmark to cofound the chapter when they realized that the new group registration process would take at least two months—and without being a registered group, they were unable to reserve rooms, get funding, set up an email list, email announcements about the group to dorm lists, or hold any activities on campus. They decided to hold an organizational meeting off campus to gauge interest and set their priorities for the year.

"We plastered the campus with signs that read, '1,140 children die every hour. Find out how you can help,' with the meeting location and time listed below," Regan said.

As a new student, I had a campus map in one hand and my flyers, tape, and a stapler in the other. Two days later, Brian and I arrived at the meeting room early, with refreshments and handouts. We sat down, watching the clock, unsure if anyone would arrive. One by one, students trickled in.

Many of the students hadn't done any work before in international health, so at the organizational meeting, Regan said, "We started by outlining the basic facts . . . the most pressing statistics, the major diseases kids die from every year, and the U.S. government's role in addressing the global burden of disease. We tried to keep the information manageable, and started a straightforward letter-writing campaign that would be easy for new students to take charge of."

One of their greatest obstacles, Regan reported, was that "people needed to acquire a great deal of information to be effective advocates and feel comfortable meeting with government officials, writing opinion pieces for the newspaper, and speaking in an educated way to their peers on campus about international children's health issues." But all the international health courses were open only to people who had completed a variety of prerequisite courses, so freshmen and sophomores were unable to take these classes.

Regan and Brian soon came up with a solution: they would teach an international health course themselves through their school's "student initiated course" program, whereby undergraduate or graduate students can petition to teach a course if the university is unable to offer it. They were off and running, Regan said, when they found two anthropology professors to sponsor them so they could teach their course for credit and be listed in the university course catalogue.

Regan and Brian taught "International Children's Health and Survival" during the fall term of their junior year. Their first class had twenty students, ranging from freshmen to seniors, who learned about different health topics each week, ranging from child nutrition to the role of poverty in disease. Professors were invited from a variety of departments to give guest lectures and facilitate discussions.

Empowered with knowledge, those new SCCS members helped the organization develop so it was able to take on larger and larger projects, like partnering with an advocacy program at the university's medical school and working with a local elementary school whose students were struggling with poor-quality nutrition.

Like Regan and Brian, exemplary student leaders seize the initiative themselves and encourage initiative in other students.

There are several ways you can create the conditions under which people will overcome their reluctance and be ready and willing to seize

> *Don't wait for your ship to come in and*
> *feel angry and cheated when it does not.*
> *Get going with something small.*
>
> —Irene Kassorla

the initiative in both calm and calamitous times. One is to hone your *out-sight*—the capacity to perceive external things—and help your group develop that ability too.

Innovations can come from anywhere, and you must actively look at and listen to what's going on around you, both on and off campus, for signs that there's something new on the horizon. This is especially true when the group is homogenous or has little diversity of thought and experience. Research has shown higher-performing groups to have significantly more communication with people outside their own groups, whether with student organizations on the same campus or with student groups or organizations off-campus and at other schools. Unless external communication is actively encouraged, people interact with outsiders less and less frequently and new ideas are cut off.

People who challenge the status quo believe they can do something about the situation they face and are more likely to act than those who do not, so student leaders must provide opportunities for people to gain mastery on a task one step at a time. Regan and Brian Bergmark started a new SCCS chapter with a straightforward letter-writing campaign and then created a forum for SCCS members and others to ask questions, debate issues, and develop over time as a community for children's health advocacy. They understood that people's confidence increases when they have the knowledge and skills to do what needs to be done—this helps people feel confident that they can act when the situation requires. As Regan, Brian, and all exemplary student leaders understand, seizing the initiative is ultimately about attitude and action, believing you can make something happen.

> *Looking up gives light, although*
> *at first it makes you dizzy.*
>
> —Rumi

It's important to remember that challenging the process is not about challenge for challenge's sake. It's not about shaking things up just to keep people on their toes. It's about challenge for meaning's sake. It's about living your life on purpose. Mountain climber Arlene Blum says, "As long as you believe what you're doing is meaningful, you can cut through fear and exhaustion and take the next step."

What gets student leaders—everyone, really—through the tough times, the scary times, the times when you don't think you can even get up in the morning or take another step, is a sense of meaning and purpose. "I would sometimes challenge my father's ways of doing things," Wilson Tsai said of his experience comanaging a struggling small family aquaculture business. "We never saw the disagreements as something negative because each of us had different perspectives and we would come to a compromise. . . . Even though starting the fish farm business was a much harder life than before, the farm life and all the responsibilities that go along with it have shaped me to become who I am today."

At its core, Challenge the Process is about innovation, and innovation requires more listening and communication than does routine work, so promoting internal communication is just as important as being open to ideas from outside the organization. Student leaders guiding change must establish more relationships, connect with more sources of information, and get out and walk around more frequently.

Stephany Sue served on the eight-person board of officers of a club that sought to bring social problems to the attention of the student body. "Our club needed to think outside of what we had always known," said Stephany.

> The people doing the presentations on the issues were the officers themselves, some of whom had no personal relation to the subject at hand. . . . They knew all the facts and all the statistics, but they didn't have the personal aspect that was needed in these meetings. Therefore, the topics didn't move the audience; they were as cool and as aloof as if they were reading a textbook on the matter.
>
> The officer-lecture process we were using wasn't working, so we had to challenge the process itself. I knew that challenging the norm wouldn't be easy, because it meant ignoring everything that our predecessors had done and it meant doing something entirely different from what the old process was. We had to completely restructure the way the club operated and the way we ran our meetings.

The board decided that the only way for the club to get the attention of the student body in a sea of competing interests was to put on speakers who had personal contact with the issue being presented. "We needed speakers who could tell intimate stories about their encounters with steroids, rape, drugs, and other issues," Stephany said.

Sometimes they had siblings or friends whom they could call on. Other times they contacted clinics for counselors on issues like STDs and drunk driving. They convinced a faculty member to come talk about his experiences as a teenager that led to his anorexia and about his experiences as a male anorexic. A recent graduate came back to talk about how she was so stressed in her junior and senior years that she had resorted to cutting and self-mutilation. A parent came to talk about his son's suicide and taught the audience how to recognize the symptoms of a suicidal person.

"The impact of these speakers was immediate," Stephany told us.

We had learned about these issues from our textbooks and from television or magazines, but the majority of the student body had never been exposed to the raw details and pure intimacy that our speakers provided. Our club roster swelled into the hundreds. People came to our meetings because they were captivated by the stories our speakers told. They could understand the struggles the speakers were going through because they themselves were going through the same difficult times: substance abuse, academic and financial pressures, the death of a family member or friend, parents' divorces, physical and mental health issues. . . . Other people were compelled to attend because they had friends or family members that were struggling with the issue. . . . Eventually, the club had to move the bimonthly meetings from our usual classroom to the union because of our boom in meeting attendance.

By looking outside their own organization, Stephany's board of officers brought a new dynamic to the way the club was perceived and run. They found a way to have people with real connection to an issue speak from the heart about their trials and difficulties.

> **Keep an open mind, but not so wide that your brains fall out.**
> —Unknown

In the process, they exemplified a key leadership truth: Leaders who are dedicated to getting extraordinary things done are open to receiving ideas from anyone and anywhere. They are adept at constantly surveying the landscape of technology, politics, economics, demographics, art, religion, and society in search of new ideas. It's by keeping the doors open to the passage of ideas and innovation that you become knowledgeable about what goes on around you.

It all boils down to keeping your eyes and ears open for new ideas, exposing yourself to broader views, and being willing to hear, consider, and accept ideas from outside your own group. Which is, after all, a major purpose of a college education in the first place. This is not to say that you have to think that you must be responsible for initiating all the change. Innovation and improvement are everyone's responsibility, and the impetus for change can come from many sources.

EXPERIMENT AND TAKE RISKS

Success in challenging the process demands more than a constant search for new ideas for changing the status quo. It also requires a willingness to take risks and experiment with innovative ideas. Of course, when you experiment, not everything works out as intended. There are mistakes and false starts. That's part of the process of innovation. What's critical, therefore, is that student leaders promote learning from these experiences. Leaders must encourage others to step into the unknown instead of playing it safe. Small, visible steps are more likely to win early victories and gain early supporters than are big-bang efforts.

To get people to want to change their existing behaviors and attempt extraordinary performance, student leaders break down big problems into small, doable steps and get people to say "yes" again and again. Small wins help them build constituents' commitment to a course of action by starting with actions that are tangible, doable, and within their control.

Small wins build students' confidence and reinforce their desire to feel successful. They provide a stable foundation that preserves gains and makes it harder to return to the way things were. They make people want to do more.

> **The secret to getting ahead is getting started.**
>
> —Sally Berger

Student leaders encourage incremental innovation and continual experimentation to help people learn and come up with new ideas. By trying lots of little things in the service of something much bigger, they continually generate lots of possibilities for small wins. And all those possibilities can add up to big results.

That's exactly what Amanda Itliong learned when she was vice president of her university's chapter of the National Society of Collegiate Scholars.

At the time that I took a leadership position with this organization it was one of those honor societies that doesn't really do much except induct students with a certain GPA, collect dues from them and then induct more people the next year. My fellow leaders and I quickly realized that our organization actually had quite a bit of money from all those years of dues collected that hadn't been spent.

We looked to the mission of our organization for ideas about what we could do with the money. Since we were founded as a group to support academics and service excellence we started to brainstorm ways that we might be able to really use our funds to make an impact on academics and service.

We decided that the arts was an area where our school didn't offer very many opportunities for students to showcase their work and that funding for community arts in our city was scarce. We came up with a plan to hold a student-created fashion and arts showcase called "Diversion" to benefit a non-profit that teaches the arts and entrepreneurship to low income kids in the area. Even though we were really excited about the plan, we knew that it was going to be difficult to get other people on board and involved in the process because our group didn't usually do anything and all of sudden we were planning a huge event.

"Planning a large arts event was definitely a big risk for us to take, since it would require a lot of approvals, support, and volunteers from a group of people who were used to our group doing nothing," Amanda told us. So her group broke the task down into lots of little pieces.

First they started a forum for people to hear about the general "dream" for the event and contribute their personal ideas to the process. They literally drew a detailed picture of the way they envisioned the auditorium during the event and included all of the possibilities of what would be there and what it could look like. Then they started working with people all over campus to find out how to connect to the interests and values of other groups and individuals that they would need for support. Little by little they got people to say "yes," again and again. As Amanda tells it:

> The Art Department quickly got on board because we included in our idea a small gallery that was open before the show and during intermission and also gave them space to advertise their academic programs to students. The multicultural groups were excited to showcase their music and dance talents while helping a local good cause at the same time too. With the input and brainstorms from so many people we were able to create a really amazing vision.

From those initial small wins, Amanda says, "We hosted a sold-out event that was fun for everyone! The arts became very visible through the event and a local charity received significant funding. Since we used the organization's saved funds for all production costs, every cent we raised through ticket sales went to the non-profit."

> **Only those who risk going too far can possibly find out how far they can go.**
>
> —T. S. Eliot

Experimenting and taking risks doesn't always play out so nicely. Student leaders report that mistakes and failures are crucial to their success because they are learning experiences. People learn by doing things they've never done before, and no one ever does anything perfectly the first time. Studies of the innovation process make the point that success is not what breeds future success. It breeds failure. It is failure that is the incubator for success.

Student leaders appreciate that the overarching objective of any innovative endeavor is *learning*. Learning happens when people feel comfortable in talking about both successes and failures, about what went right and what went wrong. Leaders don't look for someone to blame when the inevitable mistakes are made in the name of innovation. They ask instead, "What can be learned from the experience?"

Student leaders create a climate for learning that recognizes that people learn in different ways: for example, by taking action (trial and error), by reading and thinking, by feeling, and by accessing others. They know that learning requires tolerating some inefficiencies and failures. They accept the necessary trade-off between proficiency and learning.

The inevitable failures of innovation can cause stress, but stress can energize people and even generate enthusiasm and enjoyment. The key is how people respond.

> *The harder you fall, the higher you bounce.*
>
> —Chinese proverb

Student leaders who handle stress positively are psychologically hardy. Instead of being debilitated by the stress of a difficult experience, they view change as challenge and are energized by it. They have a strong sense of control, of being able to influence what is going on; a strong commitment, believing they can find something worthwhile in the situation; and a strong belief in the power of challenge. People with a hardy attitude take change, turmoil, and the strains of life in stride. They are able to transform stressful events into manageable or desirable situations.

Take it from Dan Stypa, who worked on organizing a community service trip for students from his university. As Dan explained, each year, during their three-week winter break, students volunteer "to help those in need somewhere else in the country."

For the last two years, students have gone to the Gulf Coast, to Mobile, Alabama, and New Orleans, Louisiana, to help with the ongoing Hurricane Katrina recovery efforts. In the past, this service trip was primarily planned and executed by university staff members with some students providing their input. However, this year has been completely different.

Rather than being planned by university staff members, the winter break trip is being planned by a team of six undergraduate students, including myself, being advised by a staff member. With this huge shift, our committee has been faced with many obstacles, such as less university funding, hesitation of the staff to let go, and balancing the needs of the university with the desires of the students.

Many students said that they wanted a new community service experience and did not want to go back to the Gulf Coast, so the team found a North Carolina group that would welcome their efforts. To make matters even more challenging, with much less university funding, the team had to reach out into the community to look for sponsors and engage in fundraising efforts. Between having to be creative with funding and establishing contacts with entirely new people in a group that they had never worked with, Dan's team had completely broken with what had been done in the past. "Staff members understandably had some hesitations," Dan said.

> One of the things that encountered the most resistance was choosing a new location and keeping the trip during winter break. However, by doing our homework, we were able to show the staff that we were passionate about this. All of us students on the planning committee talked with our friends and reported our findings back to the staff. In addition, we created a very detailed budget and took the initiative to get price quotes from various companies. Once staff members saw how dedicated we were to the cause, by seeing our budgets, survey results, and research into a new location, they knew that we were planning and covering all of our bases. We were not moving without direction, and they saw that we were setting goals and achieving them. This gave the staff members confidence in our abilities, and they bought into our vision of creating one of the most memorable experiences for students possible.

Like Dan and his team, you can help people cope with stressful situations by building a sense of control, by asking them to do challenging tasks that are within their skill level. You can help by encouraging other students to see change as opportunity. People have an intuitive sense of what makes them strong and what makes them weak. The challenge is to apply these lessons to daily life. Student leaders have a responsibility to create an environment that breeds hardiness on a regular basis.

REVIEW AND PRACTICE

Leadership is closely associated with change and innovation. When students—be they entrepreneurs, managers, community activists, educators, volunteers, or individual contributors, young or old people, or those at the top, middle, or bottom of the organizational pyramid—describe their personal-best leadership experiences, they talk about the challenge of change. When we look at leaders, we see that they're associated with transformations, large and small. Leaders don't have to change history, but they do have to change "business as usual."

The pace of change has accelerated, and opportunities may come and go in a nanosecond. Student leaders, therefore, are proactive: they actively seek and create new opportunities. They're always on the lookout for anything that lulls a group into a false sense of security; they constantly invite and create new initiatives. Leaders, by definition, are out in front of change, not behind it trying to catch up.

> **The secret to my success is that I bit off more than I could chew and chewed as fast as I could.**
>
> —Paul Hogan

The quest for change is an adventure. It tests your will and your skill. It's tough, but it's also stimulating. It brings forth talents that have been dormant. It introduces you to yourself. For you to get the best from yourself and others, you must understand what gives meaning and purpose to work and what makes it intrinsically motivating. External rewards aren't sufficient when you struggle for shared aspirations.

Innovation and leadership are nearly synonymous. Leaders are innovators; innovators are leaders. The focus of a leader's attention is less on the routine operations and much more on the untested and untried. Student leaders are always asking "What's new? What's next? What's better?" And when you're searching for opportunities to grow and improve, the most innovative ideas are most often not your own and not even in your own organizations. They're elsewhere, and the best leaders look all around them for the places in which breakthrough ideas are hiding. Exemplary leadership requires outsight, not just insight. That's where the future is.

A major task for all student leaders is to identify and remove self-imposed constraints and organizational conventions that block innovation and creativity. Innovation is always risky, so leaders recognize failure as a necessary fact of the innovative life. Instead of punishing it, they encourage it; instead of trying to fix blame for mistakes, they learn from them; instead of adding rules, they encourage flexibility.

Student leaders are experimenters: they experiment with new approaches to all problems. They venture outside the constraints of normal routine and experiment with creative and risky solutions. They create climates in which other students can also accept the challenge of change.

Leaders guide and channel the often-frenetic human motion of change toward some end. When things seem to be falling apart, leaders show their constituents the exciting new world they can create from the pieces. Out of the uncertainty and chaos of change, leaders rise up to show how accepting the present challenge will actually help shape a better tomorrow. This is critical to commitment levels, as people need to believe that they're dedicating themselves to the creation of a noble and meaningful future that is worthy of their best efforts.

By having and fostering an attitude of psychological hardiness, you can take the potential turmoil and stress of innovation and change it into an adventure. By creating opportunities for small wins, you make it possible for students to get started on new adventures. In establishing step-by-step ways to learn from both success and failure, you create the climate and the conditions for turning your constituents into leaders themselves.

Here are some steps to take to get started on Challenge the Process.

I. CHECK FOR LIMITING ASSUMPTIONS

It is not unusual to find that even before you start a project or assignment, there are possible limitations on what you can do. Some of the limits are real and rational and some are imaginary and emotional. Working by yourself or with others, make a list of the "I/we can't do this because . . ." statements that may constrain your project:

1.

2.

3.

4.

5.

6.

7.

Now look over your list and do the following: Put a plus (+) sign next to those statements that are true, then figure out what you are going to do about this. Put a minus (–) sign by those that are not true (or may be true but can be challenged), then think about how to handle these. Put a check (✓) next to those limiting assumptions that you definitely need to challenge in the planning and execution of your project (perhaps even *any* project).

II. LOOK OUTSIDE

The best student leaders and their organizations do not assume that they have all the ideas or answers that they need. They know that the source of creative and innovative ideas on how to do things differently is very likely to be outside of their boundaries.

Who is already doing something you think is cool, awesome, bold? What can you do to creatively build on their idea and customize it to your own circumstances? Make a list of three specific things you will do to search outside of your project or assignment to discover unexpected ideas.

1.

2.

3.

III. GET STARTED IN SMALL WAYS

Isn't there something you have been dying to do or wishing you could try? So do it! Not so easy? Then think about what it is that keeps you from taking action and focus on eliminating that obstacle (or at least working around it). What's holding you back? What do you need to do in order to build the self-confidence necessary to move outside your or your organization's comfort zone? Whose help do you need to succeed, and how can you get it? Make a commitment to take at least one step forward toward this objective in the next seven days.

Explain here what you are going to do and how this proposed first step will move you forward and enable you to take the second step:

I am going to

FURTHER REFLECTIONS

- Great leaders are great learners. Of course, you are in school to learn things that you didn't know before, but how can you apply this perspective to providing leadership in your club, team, residence hall, or workplace? Take something that you are now engaged with and go back and find out about its origins. Where did this thing, object, activity, policy come from in the first place? Who thought about it? What problem was it supposed to solve, or what opportunity was it supposed to take advantage of? Armed with this knowledge, how are things working out and what can you do to move this process further along?

- Make it easy for others involved on your team or in your project to say "yes." Make it easy to get people participating and to get their opinions heard. Lower the barriers to entry, so that the only reason for someone not getting involved is that the person doesn't want to become any more effective or successful!

- Make a list of all the things you do in your organization that fits the description "That's the way we've always done things around here!" For each of these, ask yourself, "How useful is this practice to doing our best?" If the answer is "absolutely essential," then keep it. Otherwise, find a way to change it. In a similar way, eliminate the phrase "That's the way we did it last year" from your discussions.

- One of the only ways you are going to know if you can do something or not is to do it. So volunteer for a tough assignment. Be proactive in looking for chances to stretch yourself and learn something new. Consider how you can supply those same opportunities, and support, to others you are working with.

6

ENABLE OTHERS TO ACT

"It was possibly one of the happiest moments of my life," Jaspreet Sanghera told us as he reflected on having been voted photography editor for his small school's first-ever newspaper. He had been up against many other journalism students who were as well qualified. "But *I* had been selected to be the leader of all things when it came to organizing the photography, and that was a feeling unrivaled."

After his initial euphoria wore off, Jaspreet said he began to feel slightly uneasy.

It was going to be a lot of hard work organizing and taking the pictures that would make up the issues. To make matters worse, the school had no actual photography equipment available for the use of the newspaper! It's then that I made the horrible mistake of thinking that I could handle the work load all by myself.

I figured that since I had my own camera, I would have to do the entire picture taking, just me alone. It was how I was used to doing things. I tended to take control and not allow anyone to help me, and that was what I was trying to do in this situation as well. I figured that if I wanted the first issue of the newspaper to look good, photography-wise at least, then I had to take the pictures myself. I could not possibly trust anybody with the job!

Initially things went smoothly. Whenever someone had a photo request, Jaspreet would fiddle around with his schedule and take care of it as soon as he could. It wasn't very difficult, because the stories were coming along slowly and there was not much need for pictures yet. "I actually was rather pleased with my decision to handle everything by myself," he said. "I felt like nothing could get in my way."

But then something did get in his way: the call for a full spread of photography, a photo essay. "This had not been in the job description," Jaspreet told us. "I believed I only had to take pictures that others told me to take. I had many ideas for a theme for the photo essay but none of them really seemed to work out. The main concern was the time constraint."

How was I to get together a bunch of themed pictures all nice and ready before the issue went to print? I considered asking for some assistance from someone but I came to the conclusion that if I could not figure out something then no one else could either.

Too late he discovered the leadership maxim: *You're not any more special than anybody else in this organization.* "I was not any better than my classmates at taking pictures or thinking up innovative ways to handle the photo essay," he said. "But to my dismay, I did not realize that early enough." Subsequently, the first issue went to press without any photo essay.

> I was deeply ashamed. It had been solely my fault and I could only blame myself. That's when I decided to put my ego away and ask for help for the next issue. I was not going to let that one go to print unfinished.
>
> I decided I would have to enlist the help of others who were willing *and* able to take pictures whenever a story demanded and also to help with the photo essay. And I knew just where to look. My fellow nominees for the position of photography editor had been just as qualified as I was in photography and I believed I could rely on them to help me out. . . . We needed all to work together and make sure we could get the best quality pictures. . . . Teamwork was what was going to make this issue work.

The group came up with dozens of great ideas; then they decided to ask the whole journalism department what their preferences were. "Even though the writers had little to do with photography," Jaspreet recalled, "I felt that now more than ever, everyone's opinion mattered." The winning idea was a photo essay depicting the school's many different social networks. The team of photographers went to work, and the photo essay was a big success. "People were ecstatic to have their picture taken with their best friends and then be featured in the newspaper."

Each issue thereafter was also "fantastic," Jaspreet told us, the result of the lessons he had learned in teamwork, trust, and empowerment. Collectively figuring out what needed to be done and enabling others to act "had worked out like a dream."

> The experience of being photography editor greatly changed my outlook in leadership. I felt a bit ashamed for the very many times

previously that I had overpowered a group I was working with. I always believed that I would do a much better job than any of them would and that I did not even require any help from them. But now I knew that I had always been wrong about that. . . . I realized [now] that if I asked for help and if I empowered my group-mates that everyone did a better job and accomplished a lot more. . . . One person alone can never really accomplish as much as a group of truly dedicated persons can.

What Jaspreet learned (the hard way) is that you can't do it all by yourself; you have to *enable others to act.* In our research, we have never encountered a single example of extraordinary achievement that occurred without the active involvement and support of many people. Enabling others to act is essential for getting extraordinary things done, no matter what the endeavor—a school newspaper, a campus fund drive, a winning sports season, a successful residence hall event, or building a house for Habitat for Humanity.

> **If I have seen further than others, it is because**
> **I was standing on the shoulders of giants.**
>
> —Isaac Newton

FOSTER COLLABORATION

Student leaders in all sorts of organizations tell us that today's diverse, 24×7×365 world demands even more collaboration and trust, not less. Remember Dan Stypa in Chapter Five, who organized a new community service trip at his university? Part of Dan's team's strategy was fostering collaboration, or in his words, to be "passionate about empowering others."

We built off of one another's strengths and created a team approach. The six of us had a productive discussion of why we think certain people would be best for certain positions. . . . Although everyone had unique responsibilities, we were working as a team and not afraid to ask one another for help. For example, the social chair was unsure how to contact the local university for ideas on social activities. One of the committee members agreed to help her with that aspect of the trip even though it wasn't necessarily her responsibility. Building an environment of inclusiveness and openness enabled each person to ask questions and work together.

As Dan and other exemplary student leaders know, to get extraordinary things done you must foster collaboration and create conditions whereby people know they can count on one another, by building trust and strong relationships within your group. Trust is the central issue in human relationships within and outside organizations, and it is essential for getting extraordinary things done. Student leaders who do not trust others end up doing all the work themselves, as Jaspreet did in his early days as photo editor. Or they supervise the work so closely they become overly controlling. Either way, the result is that people do not trust them.

Even when Jaspreet decided to enlist other photographers to help him with the paper's photo essay, he hit a snag. "No one really had a decent camera," he told us. "I realized that the only thing I could do was let the others borrow my precious camera when they needed it. I had to make that sacrifice. Once the camera issue was out of the way, my new photographers and I got together . . . and started brainstorming ideas for the photo essay." They were on their way to an outstanding production.

People who create distrustful environments are directive and hold tight to the reins of power, so the people working with them are likely to withhold and distort information. "When a leader does not open up to the possible suggestions of others, they are no longer leading a group of people; they are controlling them—thus shutting themselves off from the possibilities for change." So Heather McKenzie observed as she reflected on her leadership of the annual project of writing an accolade to each member of her school's graduating class. "If I had not turned this project from a small team effort into a large team effort involving every member of the junior class, the results would not have been as positive."

> We broke up into groups of four or five and divided up our classmates in alphabetical order. I did not want the other members of our team to feel that I was in any way in control of the deliberations, so I did not "oversee" the other groups. I simply joined one of the groups just as anyone else would have. I wanted to make the other members of the team feel important; I wanted them to know that I trusted them and their ideas, with the hopes that they would feel strengthened and more capable of acting on their own initiative.

Heather largely credits the great success of the project to this trust in her team members.

> **The small, brave act of cooperating with another person, of choosing trust over cynicism, generosity over selfishness, makes the brain light up with quiet joy.**
>
> —Natalie Angier

Studies show that the more trusted people feel, the better they innovate. Trust is the most significant predictor of people's satisfaction with their club, team, work group, or other organization. Trusting leaders nurture openness, involvement, personal satisfaction, and commitment to excellence. And trust begets trust.

Because they trust, exemplary student leaders consider alternative viewpoints, make use of others' expertise and influence, and let others influence group decisions. When Samantha Morrow and her best friend were asked to head a group of approximately seventy students to launch an environmental club at a local elementary school, they started writing lesson plans, planning activities, and organizing the club completely on their own.

"At the beginning of the year it was my partner and I working continuously and trying to do everything," Samantha told us. "This was disastrous. It was impossible for me and my friend to single-handedly do the amount of work such a project required." So they set out to get to know each of the other students assigned to the project well enough to suggest appropriate tasks and responsibilities. In the process of discovering what tasks were best suited to each, she said, "We developed the utmost confidence in their getting the job done."

> After trying out members of the group in different roles and actually trusting them, the stress and work load started to diminish. By the end, our group dynamic had finally been discovered and we were able to divide the responsibility in a practical and functional way. The end result was a fun and educational club that the kids loved, and my partner and I received the state-wide Youth Environmental Award for our efforts.

Some specific ways you can demonstrate trust are to listen and learn from others and share information and resources. Listening to what others have to say and appreciating their points of view demonstrates respect for them and their ideas, and people listen more attentively to those who listen to them. By consulting with others and getting them to share information, you make certain that people feel involved in making decisions that affect them.

> *He that speaks, sows; he that hears, reaps.*
>
> —Turkish proverb

Before asking for trust from others, you must demonstrate your trust in them. That means taking the risk of disclosing what you stand for, value, want, hope for, and are willing and unwilling to do.

A key lesson for Jonas Pauliukonis, when he reflected back on his personal-best leadership experience, was learning to let go and trust others. He recalled his experience becoming the leader of the Cougar Patrol—a group of eight ten- and eleven-year-olds fresh out of Cub Scouts. The Cougars were "a wild bunch," he said, "easily distracted and not prone to listening to an older Scout. Sometimes I would come home from meetings feeling discouraged and doubting my skill as a leader. At times I felt like giving up."

The turning point came when the troop was preparing for Camporee, a district-wide event at which Scouts from around the metropolitan area come together to demonstrate their skills and compete for recognition in a series of challenges.

As I continued to work with the Scouts, I found myself delegating more and more and found that as I did this they became more dependable. I created opportunities for the young Scouts to develop their skills by working together on the tasks and allowing them to practice the skills individually and as a team.

The Cougars earned the first place award for Best Patrol at Camporee. It turned out that their scores in the challenges were good, "but what really won the judges over," Jonas said, "was our joint efforts in all the competitions and Scout spirit."

The magic behind the Cougars' success lies in delegation and trust. The fact that the patrol members had ownership in the process is what allowed us to produce extraordinary results. They succeeded because they accomplished what they did as a team.

I inspired the patrol to practice Scout spirit, helped each member to recognize the skills he brought to the group, encouraged each one to do his best, and then turned the process over to the group to function as a whole. Even though no one person stood out in the patrol, the Cougars certainly stood out against the other patrols.

As Jonas and the Cougars discovered, one of the most significant ingredients of cooperation and collaboration is a sense of *interdependence*—a condition in which each member knows that he or she cannot succeed unless everyone else succeeds, or at least that they can't all succeed unless they coordinate their efforts. Without a sense of mutual dependence, it's virtually impossible to create the conditions for positive teamwork.

> **To say my fate is not tied to your fate is like saying,**
> **"Your end of the boat is sinking."**
> —Hugh Downs

No one can do it alone. For a positive experience together, students must have cooperative goals and roles. A focus on a collective purpose binds people together into cooperative efforts. Each person's job should make a contribution—tasks must be designed so that each person contributes something unique to the outcome.

Brian Reese was a college senior when the instructor in a core engineering class divided them up into groups and told them each group had to turn in a final project worth nearly 30 percent of their course grade by the end of the semester.

"The requirements were vague," Brian explained, "and all the work had to be completed by the group members alone, with no outside assistance. I decided to step up and make some suggestions, even though I didn't completely understand the technical scope of the project."

"When I first thought about leadership," Brian told us, "I imagined a truly dynamic individual who gains respect through actions over time." But in this situation, the professor had not assigned a group leader, and the students didn't have enough time in their daily schedules to meet on a regular basis and allow a leader to emerge. "The group was waiting for someone to lead," Brian said, "so I decided to take the challenge."

The challenge as Brian saw it was to find a way to divide the project up based on each member's individual strengths, while stimulating group interaction. "I decided to call one group meeting in the library at school, and soon realized the extensive knowledge possessed by other team members." Brian saw that the best way to attack the project was to enable the other team members to use their mathematical skills to develop formulas and spreadsheets, while he would handle the write-up and presentation.

He described what happened: "I wasn't sure where to start, but we started nonetheless. . . . Organizing the first meeting and enabling other group members to act made them feel important, which helped create buy-in. This was enough to get the ball rolling and eventually carry the group to the end of the semester."

People who grow up in a culture that rewards individual or competitive achievement have the perception that they'll do better if people are rewarded solely on their individual efforts. But as Brian and his fellow engineering students learned, cooperation pays bigger bonuses because people are more likely to cooperate if a project or task is structured so their *joint efforts* are rewarded. Brian said of the experience, "Enabling others is a powerful concept, and the leader must realize they may not be the smartest person with the best ideas. Recognizing the importance of working together helps foster a positive working environment that allows for group interaction to stimulate new and better ideas."

> **Gettin' good players is easy.**
> **Gettin' 'em to play together is the hard part.**
> —Casey Stengel

Student leaders know that positive face-to-face interactions are critical for collaboration to occur. There is no more effective way to build trust and promote teamwork than getting people together regularly, face to face.

"It would have been ridiculous not to take advantage of the steady stream of different ideas available from everyone, and readily give credit to everyone who contributed," Cantalina Nguyen told us in her account of serving as one of four editors on her school newspaper. To "foster a sense of camaraderie," she said, "all we had to do was be there with everyone."

Working on the paper became an obsession for me and the three other editors. Then I saw the rest of the staff get excited because we were excited, and they in turn saw us getting more enthusiastic about the work, and so on. We were all like rubber balls bouncing off the walls faster and faster the more we found to do and improve. Despite occasionally succumbing to the usual distractions like free pizza and our ever-moody printer, things went smoothly because we were able to work together.

But when there were questions or crises, the four editors were there to hack away at them for hours until we solved them. Still, we were never alone. Other staff members, wanting to keep us company, started to say, "We'll stay at lunch and come back late tonight, too," sitting at their computers until the job was done. It was beautiful in that cramped newspaper office, all of us there working together.

But what about moving projects forward when you're not physically sitting next to the people you're working with? Listen to Ben Casnocha, also a school newspaper editor and the author of *My Start-Up Life: What a (Very) Young CEO Learned on His Journey Through Silicon Valley*, describe the day his co-editor called him because she thought he was upset:

> We had been trading emails all day on school newspaper decisions. . . . What I had interpreted as a string of efficient emailing back-and-forth, she had seen as an Angry Ben expressing his displeasure and disappointment with the way things were going. In other words, due to my own imprecision and disregard for tone, my partner and I were on completely different pages, and it took a couple phone calls and meetings to get us back on track.

"Ah, email," Ben reflected later. "Some experts say the tone of at least 50 percent of emails sent is misread by the recipient. So I'm not alone in being seduced by the efficiency of virtual communication."

This is a predicament more and more college students are facing. "My generation of students is growing up super-busy and all-conquering," Ben observed. "We embody the stereotype of the 'Organization Kid,' to use the David Brooks term referring to overscheduled overachievers."

> Try organizing a club meeting while on the go from a soccer game to a drama rehearsal (with a big math test the next day on your mind). As early as in high school or college, students are trying to be leaders in time-crunched, high pressure situations.
>
> Naturally, we turn to technology to help us manage our complicated lives. More specifically we use technology to communicate with those involved in our various endeavors: instant messaging, email, cell phone, text messaging, Facebook messages, among other yet-to-be-invented forms.

How does the use of these technologies allow you to enable others to act if you're not physically with your fellow classmates and followers?

"This question—grappling with the 'communication' part of leadership, widely accepted as essential, in the specific context of email and other mediums—deserves more thought," Ben says.

> At the least, for young leaders who are always connected and trying to juggle multiple projects, learning how to write with precision seems like a most important skill. But perhaps the ultimate sign of a wise leader is knowing when to communicate through the wonderful new technologies we've grown up on, and when to resort to the slow but emotionally rich mediums our parents used when they were leading.

And how do you decide when to use the newer technologies and when to go the old but more "emotionally rich" route? Ben's advice:

> First, I think about the person with whom I'm communicating. If I know s/he is technologically-inclined, I'll more quickly employ email. Second, I think about the issue at hand. Most trivial matters involving logistics, dates, numbers, etc., are best done with email or web tools. A performance review, on the other hand, is better suited to an "emotionally rich" medium. Tech obviously offers efficiency first and foremost. Also, *tone* is hugely important. The smiley face emoticon in email can be overused, but can be effective at softening tone. In in-person or phone conversations, I find people too quickly fall into an accusing tone. People hate being "accused" of anything.

As Ben's experience shows and Cantalina's newspaper staff proved, ongoing interaction promotes people's positive feelings for one another and is more likely to produce collaboration. You need to provide opportunities for people to get together, because positive face-to-face interaction has a powerful influence on whether goals are achieved. "Leadership isn't a place; it's a process," Cantalina reminded us. "Everyone pulled together in a 'process' to put together a paper we were proud to distribute each month."

> *In organizations, real power and energy is generated through relationships. The patterns of relationships and the capacities to form them are more important than tasks, functions, roles, and positions.*
>
> —Margaret Wheatley

One more point: even though many relationships won't last after graduation, or even past the current term, every significant relationship should be treated as if it will last a lifetime and will be important to your future success and the success of those around you. Human networks make things happen, and the best leaders are in the middle of them. Student leaders need to invest time and effort in building and nurturing a web of relationships.

STRENGTHEN OTHERS

As part of enabling others to act, student leaders need to instill confidence in their fellow students and help them recognize their own abilities. Exemplary leaders *strengthen others*. They enable constituents to take ownership of and responsibility for their group's success by enhancing their competence and their confidence in their abilities, by listening to their ideas and acting on them, by involving them in important decisions, and by acknowledging and giving credit for their contributions.

Creating a climate in which people are fully engaged and feel in control of their own lives is at the heart of strengthening others. People must have the latitude to make decisions based on what they believe should be done. They must work in an environment that both develops their abilities to perform a task or complete an assignment and builds a sense of self-confidence. They must hold themselves personally accountable for results as well as feel ownership for their achievements.

David Chan Tar Wei, reflecting on his experience of inaugurating a new "house system" at his college, observed, "While it is always tempting to instruct and direct one's desired course of action to someone else, the challenge lies in being able to not only inspire others to act but to enable them to do so, by providing them the support and space to do so." He explains,

> That was something I felt rather strongly about—after all, it would seem inherently contradictory to dictate, top-down, a system that was aimed to achieve diversity and vibrancy. I hoped that each house captain would truly be a great leader in his or her own way, and in so doing achieve our final vision. The house captains were given the full space to lead the directors and members of their houses. Even with all that latitude, I believe that it is necessary to enable others to act by supporting them, helping them search for any required resources and taking care of perhaps little details that may be forgotten or neglected.
>
> But essentially, I guess the most sincere and effective way to enable another to act is to share one's experiences in the hope that others will learn from them and either implement them or avoid them—just as I had tried to do, being a former house captain, by mentoring the current captains.

Student leaders accept the paradox of power: *They become most powerful when they give their power away.* "Turning our senior accolade-writing process into a larger team effort built upon trust and confidence was a bit of a risk," Heather McKenzie observed, "but one that was worthwhile to take. . . . When I gave away my power, allowing others to act, I ensured a successful outcome."

> **I must follow the people. Am I not their leader?**
>
> —Benjamin Disraeli

Shared power results in higher performance and greater fulfillment for any group. Student leaders who share power demonstrate profound trust in and respect for others' abilities, and those people become more committed to carrying out their responsibilities: they own their role, their job, their function within the group.

What is called *empowering* is really just liberating people to use the power and skills they already have, expanding their opportunities to use themselves in service of a common and meaningful purpose. Remember Regan Bergmark, who started a new chapter of the Student Campaign for Child Survival? "As we expanded," she told us, "I began to spend most of my time helping others develop their leadership skills and take on bigger projects. I found that, in many cases, the best way to lead was to inspire others and help them to become competent leaders in the movement for global health." As all exemplary student leaders like Regan know, any leadership practice that increases another's sense of self-determination, self-confidence, and personal effectiveness makes that person more powerful and greatly enhances the possibility of success.

Self-determination can be enhanced in a number of ways. One way is to give people more choice and autonomy. Students can lead and make a difference only if they have choice.

For higher levels of performance and greater initiative, you need to find ways for students to exercise independent judgment and make decisions on their own. With this increased discretion comes an increased ability to use and expand their talents, training, and experience.

The power to choose and exercise discretion rests on the willingness to be held accountable. The more freedom of choice people have, the more personal responsibility they must accept. It's also true that people will be more confident in doing their part when they believe others will do theirs. And the more people believe that everyone else is taking responsibility for their parts of the job—and has the competence to do it— the more trusting and the more cooperative they're going to be.

Unless students take personal responsibility and unless they are held accountable for their own actions, other students are not very inclined to want to work with them nor much inclined to cooperate in general. Individual accountability is critical to collaborative effort. All members have to do their parts for a group to function effectively. Personal accountability increases when people know their peers are counting on them. Part of a student leader's job is to set up conditions that enable every team member to feel a sense of ownership of the whole job.

Choice, discretion, and accountability fuel people's sense of power and control over their lives. Yet as necessary as enhancing self-determination is for strengthening others, it's not enough. Without the knowledge, skills, information, and resources to do a job well, without feeling competent to skillfully execute the choices that it requires, people feel overwhelmed and disabled.

> **Confidence is going after Moby Dick in a rowboat**
> **and taking the tartar sauce with you.**
> —Zig Ziglar

When people don't feel competent or confident, they are reluctant to exercise their knowledge, in part because they don't know how to perform the critical tasks and in part out of fear of being punished for making mistakes. Here's where exemplary student leaders step in and shine.

Consider Santiago Herrera, who led his polo team to a championship match in Argentina. Santiago was not the best polo player in the group, but he was judged to have the skills to lead the team because of his experience as a player since he was eight years old, living on a polo pony farm outside Bogota, Colombia.

> My self-confidence, which is an important factor in high-risk sports, was passed to my teammates. It's your attitude towards everything you do and those small talks with your teammates that make the difference. When one of them makes a mistake let them know but don't let them feel ashamed of themselves or lose their self-confidence. This can cause resentment towards the team.
>
> I would try to encourage the team no matter the circumstance, even when they made mistakes. . . . When a teammate is down on himself/herself the whole team is down; we rely on each other and we have to make it through together as a team.

To help strengthen others. student leaders also know to organize work to build up constituents' skills and experience. You share information and resources with constituents, giving people access to as much information as possible so they can hone and develop their skills and competencies. You also give constituents important opportunities to put their talents to good use by placing them at the center of solving critical problems and contributing to key goals, letting them figure out what needs to be done.

Remember Brian Reese's group assignment in his engineering course? Before he took it on, he said, he didn't really understand the technical aspects of the project and wasn't sure how to start. By calling that first meeting in the library, he came up with an effective way to engage his whole team in the project.

By creating a structure for each student to play a key role in completing the project, Brian not only built trust by having his classmates figure out what was needed but also tapped into a larger pool of talent for getting the job done. The final results were a testament to his skill in strengthening others: "We ended up with a 97 percent average on the project—quite respectable, considering that initially we didn't even know where to start!"

Student leaders also develop people's capabilities and foster self-confidence by coaching, helping them learn how to use their skills and talents and to learn from experience. In recounting his experience of coaching newcomers to his university's debate team, Gregory Smith told us, "Leadership is about finding the need and filling it for the betterment of the group. . . . I led practice every Thursday night, working with anyone who wanted to improve by encouraging and giving feedback. . . ."

In the coaching relationship, you make a lasting difference. Coaching, educating, enhancing self-determination, and otherwise sharing power with others demonstrates profound trust in and respect for others' abilities. When you help others to grow and develop, that help is reciprocated. People who feel capable of influencing their leaders are more strongly attached to those leaders and more committed to effectively carrying out their responsibilities.

REVIEW AND PRACTICE

You can't do it alone is the mantra of exemplary student leaders—and for good reason. You simply can't get extraordinary things done by yourself. You have to enable others to act in concert with you to accomplish whatever your task or project or goals may be.

Collaboration is the master skill that enables teams, partnerships, and other alliances to function effectively. Collaboration can be sustained only when you create a climate of trust and facilitate effective long-term relationships among your constituents. To get extraordinary things done, you have to promote a sense of mutual dependence—feeling part of a group in which all know that they need the others to be successful. Without that sense of "we're all in this together" it's virtually impossible to keep effective teamwork going.

Trust is the lifeblood of collaborative teamwork. To create and sustain the conditions for long-lasting connections, you have to be able to trust others and others have to trust you. Without trust you cannot lead. Without trust you and your team cannot get extraordinary things done. So share information and resources freely with your team, show that you understand their needs and interests, open up to their influence, make wise use of their abilities and expertise, and—most of all—demonstrate your trust in others before asking for them to trust you.

Student leaders embrace the challenge of facilitating relationships among all the people involved in any undertaking, ensuring that all appreciate their *inter*dependence more than any one member's independence. Cooperative goals and roles contribute to a sense of collective purpose, and the best incentive for others to work to achieve shared goals is their knowing that you'll reciprocate, helping them in return. Help begets help, just as trust begets trust. Extraordinary leaders go to great lengths to get people interacting. They know there's no such thing as virtual trust, so they encourage face-to-face interactions as often as possible to reinforce the durability of relationships and enhance interpersonal team dynamics.

To enable others to act, student leaders help them develop competence and confidence. You need to make certain that constituents have the necessary data and information to understand how the committee,

> *Any human anywhere will blossom in a*
> *hundred unexpected talents and capacities simply*
> *by being given the opportunity to do so.*
>
> —Doris Lessing

the group, or the organization operates, gets results, and does good work. Create a learning climate and coach people on how to put what they know into practice, stretching and supporting others to do more than they might have imagined possible. Use your power in service of others because you know how well capable and confident people perform. As constituents increase their competencies, even further amounts of power and discretion can be extended.

Here are some activities to help you get started in Enable Others to Act.

I. GENERATE POWER

Leaders make other people feel strong and confident. Think about a time when, as a direct result of something said or done by a leader (who could be a teacher, coach, parent, or colleague), you were made to feel personally powerful and capable. Write down those remarks and/or actions and be as specific as you can:

Now think about a time when you felt powerless, weak, and insignificant as a result of something a leader said or did. Write down what, specifically, that individual said or did:

Finally, recall a time when you were part of a project or team that just clicked—a time when it seemed that everyone was working together smoothly and effortlessly. Describe how people acted toward one another and what the team leader did that contributed to making the team work so well.

Using the lessons from your own experiences just recorded (as both an individual and as a team member), ask yourself, "How can I enable others to feel powerful and avoid diminishing their personal effectiveness? How can I contribute to teamwork and trust?" Record your responses:

II. LEARN TO DELEGATE

Blinding flash of the obvious: Everything can't be done by you alone. And the leadership paradox is that *leaders turn their followers into leaders.* Combining these insights, to accomplish the extraordinary you need to learn how to let go and find ways to enable your teammates to take on new challenges and responsibilities.

But the prevailing tendency of student leaders, in particular, is to hang on and try to do everything themselves. List the reasons you think explain why people (maybe even you) don't delegate.

By the way, what do you believe are the reasons why you *should* delegate?

Recalling your own experiences with leaders who handed off tasks and assignments effectively, what three or four actions do you believe are essential in enabling others to be successful?

1.

2.

3.

4.

III. ASK QUESTIONS, LISTEN, AND TAKE ADVICE

Leadership is a relationship, and a good relationship is based on trust. Trust is fostered by listening and attending to the other person. Trust is fostered as well by self-disclosure and a willingness to be open to new ideas and experiences.

Imagine that you are going to be meeting with the members of your team at the start of some new project or assignment. List the five or six questions you would want to be sure to ask them:

1.

2.

3.

4.

5.

6.

Why are the questions you've selected important to ask?

FURTHER REFLECTIONS

- Teamwork and trust can be built only when people interact with one another, informally as well as formally. Find ways to increase interaction among the people you are working with.

- Leadership is a team effort, not an individual effort. For the next two weeks, commit to replacing the word *I* with *we*. *We* is an inclusive word that signals a commitment to collaboration and teamwork. Use *we* liberally.

- Focus on gains, not losses. When working with others, find the areas of agreement first, rather than the differences. Explain how your colleagues have more to gain by working together than they can expect from working alone or in competition with one another.

- Be concerned about growing leadership talent in your organization. Don't just think about what will be happening on your watch; be attentive to what will happen when your term is over (like, when you graduate). Start giving others the opportunity now, before they are in charge, to learn alongside you about how things are done and what it takes to lead others. Think about being not just a role model, but also an active mentor as you move forward in real time.

ENCOURAGE
THE HEART

"I don't have the skills or coordination to dribble gracefully or shoot a perfect jump shot," Sarah Berg told us.

> No matter. I've always loved playing the sport. The combined exhilaration of fast-breaking down the court, executing plays and fighting other players for the rebound is as unpredictable as it is rewarding. It brings together a group of women for a common goal and tests them both mentally and physically to be the best they can be, and not just as an individual player but as a team unit.

Sarah had such an infectious enthusiasm for the game and strong belief in the team—plus she was competitive and hardworking—that in just her second year on the team she became one of its cocaptains.

"Captains are responsible for encouraging, inspiring, and pushing the team through her words, and most importantly her actions, to achieve a closer integration of mind, body, and soul," Sarah said. "I focused on the heart of the team."

> Instead of focusing on my shortcomings as a player, I focused on the efforts and strengths of my teammates. If someone was a good shooter I would encourage her to shoot. If they were hardworking I would praise them for that extra sprint they put in down the court. . . . In my eyes every little improvement was a victory.

Her first year as a cocaptain, Sarah told us, she concentrated on setting high expectations for the team and herself.

> One of the things I stressed the most was for every player on the team to appreciate the accomplishments of their teammates. Before home games I would write notes to each of the players, telling them what I thought they contributed to the team and wishing them luck. I would sometimes include quotes about how important the heart of the team really was.

Even when Sarah didn't get many minutes of play, she was working hard. "I made it my responsibility to push the starters as hard as I could in practice and to encourage them during games," she told us. "I was always there with praise for a good shot or nice block-out or great effort."

And that's not all Sarah did to encourage the team through her three years of leading the team. She made it a point to pay attention and offer personal encouragement to each player on the team.

> More than just focusing on the athletic side of the team, I would connect to my teammates on a personal level as well. If someone

was having a bad day, I would ask her what was wrong and try to cheer her up with a smile or a joke. . . . By taking the time to talk to the players individually I think it made all the difference in how much effort they put into the team.

Sarah and her cocaptains also came up with ways to celebrate people's accomplishments publicly. For instance, Sarah said, "We had a system of recognition that would give awards for outstanding achievement in a game; for example, for scoring especially high points or getting a certain number of rebounds or steals. We would treat these awards as a little personal trophy for working hard in the game."

Sarah took it upon herself to make sure each player enjoyed being there, felt comfortable, and had fun playing on the team.

We made every season a season of laughs and camaraderie. . . . We would organize activities outside of practice to all hang out so that we could be together as a team in a more relaxed setting. We had team dinners, and outings, and swim parties. We would make up songs and dances to perform for the team to make them laugh and had ongoing team jokes. . . . We would always be very serious and competitive come game time, but during practices and before games we were goofy and made sure everyone was having a good time. No one wants to try hard and put a lot into something if they don't enjoy it and aren't having fun.

Looking back, Sarah said the most crucial thing in leading her team was that "I cared about my team, focusing on the heart of it all. Everyone gave their best effort without worrying about failing, because as captains we supported them no matter what. Whether they played the best game of their life, or had the hardest time even running down the court, we loved them and believed in their abilities."

As Sarah and her cocaptains discovered, caring is at the heart of leadership. To work intensely, put in long hours, and persist for months at a demanding pace, people need encouragement. They need emotional fuel to replenish their spirits. Exemplary student leaders like Sarah know this: they need to *encourage the heart* of their team by recognizing people's contributions and celebrating the group's values and victories.

RECOGNIZE CONTRIBUTIONS

Recognition is about acknowledging good results and reinforcing positive performance, shaping an environment in which everyone's contributions are noticed and appreciated. Recognition can spur people to give their personal best whenever extraordinary effort is needed. It starts with expecting the best, setting high expectations for yourself and your team.

> *Big thinking precedes great achievement.*
>
> —Wilfred Peterson

Extraordinary student leaders understand that expectations have a way of becoming self-fulfilling prophecies. Expectations are powerful because they are the frame into which people fit reality. People are likely to see what they expect to see even if it differs from what's occurring— and are likely to act in ways that are consistent with their expectations. If you expect them to fail, they probably will; if you expect them to succeed, they probably will. For example, if you don't expect to do well in a course, you will probably not study very hard and—no surprise—your performance will suffer.

"Inspiring my teammates to want to improve and play hard was a critical part of leading them," Kelsey Fulton said about her experience as captain of her volleyball team.

People were often exhausted from waking up at 6 A.M. for practice and being loaded with assignments and other activities. I had to find a way to make people try hard and be alert despite this disadvantage. . . . At the beginning of each season I would explain to my teammates that I expected them to try their hardest at all times. I showed them how important this was to me, and I knew they listened because they would feel bad about not meeting my expectations.

Expectations play an important role in developing people and drawing out their highest potential. Even though people may be anxious about going out and delivering their personal best, high expectations make them willing and excited about the challenges they face.

To produce the behavior that leads to success, students must first see themselves as capable and successful. Being clear about what you expect of them and what you're trying to accomplish is essential to helping people stay the course, especially when the going gets tough.

That's the way Nicole Jones, in her service learning project, encouraged the hearts of kids and teens with various disabilities who were learning to ride and work with horses at Little Bits Therapeutic Riding Center.

Since many of the kids were nervous about their first time riding, I was able to share my joyful experience of dealing with horses and enlighten them of the miracles and turnarounds of previous students I helped to teach. I also put myself in their situation to understand their difficulties and help them overcome their fears. Lastly, I aimed towards optimism to make the lessons an enthusiastic and fun experience for the riders.

Along the way, she would give riders praise to let them know they were doing a good job and to show them they were capable of finishing a task. Because she let them know that she believed they could develop the confidence and skill to ride, she said, "The students looked forward to the show at the end session to earn rewards and show off their amazing victories."

> *A master can tell you what he expects of you.*
> *A teacher, though, awakens your own expectations.*
> —Patricia Neal

For people to give their all, you need to focus positive expectations on outcomes and make sure that there are some consistent norms about how the game is played. Goals and values provide people with a set of standards that concentrates their efforts. *Standards* refer to both shorter-term goals and the longer-term values that form the basis for goals. Values set the stage for action, while goals release the energy, helping people experience "flow"—that ideal state in which people feel pure enjoyment and effortlessness in what they do. Ideally, people set their own goals; the leader's job is then to make sure constituents know why what they're doing is important and what end it's serving.

People are motivated to perform well when they have a challenging goal *and* receive feedback on their progress. Clear goals and detailed feedback help people become self-correcting, understand their place in the big picture, determine what they need from others, and see who might benefit from their assistance.

Take it from Gregory Smith, who accepted a leadership role in coaching the debate team at his university. The team had grown so fast that it didn't have enough coaches to help all the students prepare and compete. The two seniors on the team stepped in to assist by teaching and encouraging the younger competitors. Gregory was also selected to teach an undergraduate-level speaking class and lead the debate team's weekly practice sessions, where he became a "source of positive encouragement," he told us.

One of the greatest needs I filled on my team was being a sounding board for teammates—whether critiquing an event, or just listening and encouraging teammates with their problems, because even non-speech problems can distract them from their best performance or infect the team when ignored.

Gregory acknowledged, "I am certainly not alone in seeing and acting on this need on my team." He credits the team's high motivation and "willingness to work together" as elements that "catapulted us from being a mediocre team to being one of the best in the country."

Alex Bon learned the value of encouraging positive feedback among his golf team's members the year he made the team as a walk-on and then stepped into the role of its "emotional leader, keeping us all on track and together as we strove to reach our goals.

"The first essential element of encouraging the heart is recognizing the contributions of all the members of your team, no matter how small or seemingly unessential to the overall process," Alex said. He explained why this was particularly important for the golf team:

Since only five members of the team are actually playing in tournaments, the other six need to contribute in other ways, ranging from physically showing up and supporting/coaching teammates at tournaments, to giving positive feedback and criticism on the course . . . or even something as small as a good-luck phone call the night before a match.

To help reward the team for making these small yet meaningful contributions, Alex created a counter system:

> Each player is given a certain number of points for each birdie, eagle, or other golf course achievement but earns relatively more points for showing up at a tournament to support teammates, or going out of their way to help someone else on the team.
>
> The team MVP is decided now in this way by these points, and not by just their golf performance, making it even more valuable for every member to contribute, and rewarding the ones who do. From our number one player to the eleventh guy on the team, everyone feels good about their role and knows that they are just as important a piece in the puzzle as the rest of us.

Alex concluded, "One of the most crucial aspects of good leadership is good feedback. A job well done without positive feedback often sabotages the morale of whoever did it."

> *There is more hunger for love and appreciation in this world than for bread.*
>
> —Mother Teresa

Providing a clear sense of direction along with feedback encourages people to do their best. Rachael Dickey, community facilitator in one of her university's residential learning communities, told us, "When residents asked for my help, I would always start by letting them know about something that I thought they were already doing that was special and praise them for it. When I recognize what people are doing well, and let them know how much I and others appreciate their talents and efforts, they seemed to feel encouraged and want to work even harder because they were proud that their good work had been noticed."

Encouragement is positive information that tells people they are making progress, are on the right track, and are living up to the standards. It shows that you care and strengthens trust. But recognition is too often predictable, routine, and impersonal. Personalizing recognition sends the signal that the leader took the time to notice achievements and makes certain that others realize you are paying attention to behaviors that are consistent with shared values.

Like Rachael, David Braverman learned that you need to pay attention to the people you are working with and not only figure out what word of encouragement each person needs but also make certain everyone knows they are part of a team. Between his junior and senior years, David supervised a group of tomato pickers older than he was on his father's organic farm in Iowa. During some of the hottest parts of the summer, he told us, "when people are tired and demoralized they need to be picked up and encouraged." He kept an eye out for when people were becoming lethargic because of the heat and monotony of the work and found a way to lift each person's spirits, sometimes just by a smile or a word or two of encouragement, or by giving them an early break.

> *The first responsibility of a leader is to define reality. The last is to say thank you.*
>
> —Max DePree

"I have learned over the years that it isn't the size of the gesture that is important, but the simple fact that you noticed someone's contributions," William Hwang reminded us. At the non-profit that he founded dedicated to opening the world of science, engineering, and medicine to underprivileged children, recognition ranges from acknowledgments in publicly distributed materials like conference and journal papers, brochures, the Web site, and so forth to specific thank-yous in emails to the group. "I also apply to have each of our volunteers recognized with the President's Volunteer Service Award at our university," William said.

Spontaneous, unexpected rewards—such as a sincere word of thanks, public praise, and small gifts—are often more meaningful than formal rewards such as awards and certificates. When Pierce Cavallero was coaching an American Youth Soccer Organization team of seven-year-olds, he came up with a way to reward the kids for doing well in drills: "I would let the kid who scored the most goals wear a 'special' sweat band during the scrimmage at the end of practice."

Or take another example from freshman golf team walk-on Alex Bon:

In golf especially, as any mental game coach will tell you, positive self-feedback is crucial after every shot; I figured positive feedback from others could be even more helpful, as we are teammates, and what are we there for if not to help each other get better? I am talkative naturally on the course, and always compliment other players, and when my teammates seemed to like my constant feedback I decided it was time for a change in our normal practice routine. I told my team to utilize each other on the course as a positive third party, something that our nearly silent practice rounds of the past were heavily lacking. Even just a "good shot," "nice swing," or even a "nice try" . . . has a huge ability to restore one's confidence and keep them going.

It is amazing now to watch us play and practice, because in a foursome, after every single shot, each player has three positive comments coming their way from teammates, guaranteed. I praise teammates for good grades, good rounds, good shots, even things like good outfits, because it all makes a difference in my mind. When the other ten of my best friends follow suit, it is a powerful thing and something that has allowed us to work through the problems and emerge stronger and closer than ever.

There are few more basic needs than to be noticed, recognized, and appreciated for your efforts, so student leaders are always looking for ways to make people feel like winners. Personalizing recognition means finding the acknowledgment and reward that is special and unique for a specific individual. When Siddarth George was captain of his school's cricket team, it was often as simple as having one-on-one time with his teammates:

> I used to buy sodas or ice cream for players after training sessions, if I felt the individual had done well during training, and tried to have a one-to-one conversation with the player—emphasizing what I thought was really admirable. Personal commendation shows that the captain is paying attention and that he appreciates your extra effort. Also, it is important that the player knows why he was commended. This reemphasizes cherished team values and encourages people to consciously practice them.

To make recognition personally meaningful, you have to get to know your constituents and be creative about ways to show you care about them. With all the teaching and coaching he was doing with his debate team, Gregory Smith saw it as a matter of "building communication bridges." "I learned to monitor my method of communication and change my vocabulary, rate of talk, and even how I frame issues, depending on whom I was talking to," he told us.

Another way that leaders show they care is by paying attention and noticing what people are doing right. When leaders pay attention and show they care, they demonstrate they are genuinely interested in seeing others succeed; when people are in the presence of a caring leader, they want to show the best in themselves. Kelsey Fulton recalled about leading her volleyball team, "I found that if I congratulated a teammate for running or diving for a ball, even if they didn't get it, they would make the same, or even more, effort next time around. My teammates would continue trying hard no matter what happened."

"I was able to connect with every player on the team," Mark Soares reflected on his experience as one of the youngest and least-experienced members of his water polo team.

> I would encourage the bench players to cheer hard for the team and I was always the first player to help someone out of the pool when they needed a substitution. I was waiting there to give them a high five and tell them to keep up the good work . . . My encouragement and care for the team was genuine. I would not lie to players about their talents or how they were playing in a game. If something went wrong I would explain the problem and tell them how they would do it correctly next time. They knew I was not "b.s.-ing" them in my encouragement and it made them better performers.

> ### Know thyself to know others,
> ### for heart beats like heart.
>
> —Chinese proverb

People are more willing to follow someone they like and trust. To be trustworthy, you must trust and be open both with and to others. That means talking about your hopes and dreams, family and friends, interests and pursuits—telling people the same things you'd like to know about them. You also need to understand and see things from other people's perspectives. Listening with your eyes and your heart requires a deep level of paying attention and understanding, and it can't be done from a distance. It means, as Kelsey Fulton told us, "putting my whole heart and attention into everything."

> When giving someone a high five for a job well done, or a pat on the back for effort well made, I always made sure it came from my heart. I knew if it wasn't heartfelt it would have no meaning at all. . . . My teammates were smart individuals and could see through me if I wasn't honest, so I always had to show them compassion and honesty in everything I did. . . . I encouraged my teammates' heart through using my whole heart to congratulate, motivate, comfort, and understand their problems.

Personalizing recognition requires knowing what's appropriate individually and culturally. Rather than assuming that you naturally know what's right for others, take some time to inquire and observe. Exemplary student leaders know that, uncomfortable or embarrassing as it may seem at first to recognize someone's efforts, it's really not difficult to do. And it's well worth the effort to make a connection with each person. Leaders learn from many small and often casual acts of appreciation what works for each of their constituents and how best to encourage their hearts.

CELEBRATE THE VALUES AND VICTORIES

At the other end of the spectrum from individual, personalized recognition are celebrations—those significant occasions on which respect and gratitude are proclaimed publicly. Celebrations renew your group's sense of community and recall the values and history that bind you together.

In acknowledging community ("common unity"), student leaders create a sense of belonging and team spirit, building and maintaining the necessary social support, especially in stressful times. Remember David Chan Tar Wei, whose personal-best leadership experience was working on changing from a faculty system to a house system of governance and culture at his junior college? Reflecting on those days, David told us, "Being a leader really is not about completing the task per se but in the relationships one builds and the lives one touches and impacts."

> Our house system developed itself as a core component of my school's culture and tradition—through the creation of distinctive symbols such as the house crest, motto, animal, and shirts that people can identify themselves with. Through the successful organization of various collaborative events and the establishment of the inter-house championships, the five new houses have come to the point where friendly competition has led to the creation of an increased sense of belonging not only to the house itself but also to the school, which is indeed heartening. The house captains themselves were passionately charged up to rally their houses in a show of inter-house rivalry and competition—something that they did not just profess but truly believed from their hearts. And as the rest of the school saw their enthusiasm and passion, they naturally become charged up for their houses in their own unique way.

The best leaders know that every gathering of a group is a chance to renew commitment. Celebrations, ceremonies, and similar events offer opportunities to communicate and reinforce the actions and behaviors that are important in realizing shared values and goals. Celebrations also provide social support.

Cricket team captain Siddarth George created a Player of the Season award to honor exceptional performance throughout the season. "It was presented at the annual general meeting, where all team members

> *Celebrate what you've accomplished, but raise*
> *the bar a little higher each time you succeed.*
>
> —Mia Hamm

and coaches are present," he said. "This collectively celebrated good performance while extolling the exceptional individual."

As Siddarth knew, everything about a celebration should be matched to its purpose. You should make explicit the connections between shared values and actions that exemplify the values, and link principles to practices in a way that's memorable, motivating, and uplifting. For celebrations to work, they must be honest expressions of commitment to certain key values and the hard work and dedication of people who have lived those values.

Public celebrations of accomplishment build commitment because they make people's actions visible to their peers and therefore difficult to deny or revoke. They also help to strengthen commitment of the people involved by increasing their visibility. You should take advantage of the way public celebrations remind people that we're all in this together and dependent on one another. They reinforce the fact that it takes a group of people working together with a common purpose in an atmosphere of trust and collaboration to get extraordinary things done.

When Heather McKenzie led her school's annual tradition of writing an accolade to each member of the graduating class, the best decision she made, she told us, was to form project teams that more accurately represented the population of the junior class. "Breaking up the team into smaller groups fostered an environment of trust, empowerment, and mutual respect," she said. When the teams came back together as a large group for three final lunch-hour meetings, they "truly worked as a team by collaborating and making the final decision" for each person's accolade.

During the final meeting, I ordered pizza and we celebrated the success of our lunchtime meetings. Not only had our team succeeded in a large and difficult task, we had also bonded and became much better friends in the process . . . I believe that I used myself as an instrument of change in creating a more effective process, but I also helped produce more positive results, as seen in the happiness of my classmates.

Besides celebrating together, one of the most significant ways in which student leaders show that they appreciate the efforts of their constituents is to be out there with them. Leaders are out and about all the time. They walk around the halls, attend meetings, go to parties, sit on the bench, and show up at awards ceremonies (even when they're not on the receiving end). Being this accessible will make you more real, more genuine, more approachable, and more human. It helps you stay in touch with what's really going on. And it puts your proverbial money where your mouth is about the values you and your constituents share. Credibility goes up when student leaders are personally involved.

Celebration and community, however, will have a significant impact only when they're genuine. Elaborate productions that lack sincerity are more entertainment than encouragement. Many people say that they don't need or want recognition from someone they don't respect, or in front of people they don't feel a connection with. This underscores the importance of getting everyone involved in the celebrations. Personalizing recognitions is even more crucial when it comes to encouraging the heart.

REVIEW AND PRACTICE

Exemplary student leaders have high expectations of themselves and of their constituents. Their goals and standards are clear and help people focus on what needs to be done. Leaders provide clear directions, feedback, and encouragement. They expect the best of people and create self-fulfilling prophecies about how ordinary people can produce extraordinary actions and results. By maintaining a positive outlook and providing motivating feedback, student leaders stimulate, rekindle, and focus people's energies and drive. These are all essential to encouraging the heart of your constituents.

Leaders recognize and reward what individuals do to contribute to the group's vision and values. And they express their appreciation far beyond the limits of formal ways of giving recognition. Leaders enjoy being spontaneous and creative in saying thank you, whether by sending notes, handing out personalized prizes, singing songs, listening without interrupting, or trying any of a myriad number of other forms of recognition.

Personalizing recognition requires knowing what's appropriate both individually and culturally. Rather than assuming that you naturally know what would be valued by others, spend time observing and talking about this with others. Student leaders know that however uncomfortable or awkward they may feel about recognizing someone else's efforts and accomplishments, it's not that difficult to do—and that it's well worth the effort to connect with each person. Learn from the many small and often casual acts of appreciation what works for each constituent and how best to personalize recognition.

Celebrating together reinforces the fact that extraordinary performance is the result of many people's efforts. By celebrating people's accomplishments visibly and in group settings, you create community and sustain team spirit. By basing celebrations on consistency with key values and attainment of critical milestones, you reinforce and sustain people's focus.

Student leaders make it a point to get personally involved in celebration and recognition, demonstrating that encouraging the heart is something everyone should do. They also tell stories about individuals who have made exceptional efforts and achieved phenomenal successes. The story makes people's achievements memorable in ways that they hadn't envisioned, and provides a role model for others to emulate. Communicating a sense of appreciation in these ways for the group's work together is what encouraging the heart is all about.

> *The universe is made of stories, not of atoms.*
>
> —Muriel Rukeyser

One more important point: Encouraging the heart doesn't have to come at the end of a season or the conclusion of a project. It also doesn't have to come after you've done everything else a leader does. It's not the end of the process; it's a continuous part of the leadership journey. You can recognize contributions and celebrate your values and victories at any time, anywhere. So do it! Give courage, spread joy, and show you care about people and the work they are doing together all along the way.

Try these activities to get started on Encourage the Heart.

I. MY MOST MEANINGFUL RECOGNITION EXPERIENCE

Think back over the times when someone has personally recognized and rewarded you for a job well done. These are the times when someone showed genuine appreciation for what you accomplished. Select one time that you would consider your most memorable recognition experience and write a short story about that experience. What made this time so memorable? Why did you recall or select it? What did the person do to recognize you? Describe the setting, the person's actions, and your feelings. Write the story in as much vivid detail as you can muster.

II. TELL A GREAT STORY

Leaders are great storytellers. Stories put a human face on success; they tell us that someone just like us can make it happen. They create organizational role models that everyone can relate to, and they put behavior in a real context. Stories make the goals of the project and the values that guide the team come alive. By telling a story in detail, student leaders illustrate what everyone needs to do to live by the values and move toward the goals. They communicate the specific and proper actions that need to be taken to resolve tough choices and work strenuously. Stories bring people together "around a campfire" to learn and to have fun.

Recall a time when you observed one or more members of your team contributing to the project or organization's values and goals (this can be in a past or current setting). The following five steps guide you through how to write a story. When you have finished, look for an opportunity to tell the story.

1. *Identify the actors.* Name the person or the people you want to recognize.

2. *Paint the scene.* Where and when did this happen? What were the circumstances?

3. *Describe the actions.* Relate in as much detail as you can what happened and what this person or each person involved did.

4. *Tell how it ended.* Never leave your audience hanging. What happened as a result of the actions?

5. *Include a surprise.* Every great story includes some kind of surprise—perhaps an element of amazement. What makes this story
particularly interesting, unique, memorable, funny, or surprising?
What's an opportunity coming up for you to tell this story?

III. BUILD SOCIAL SUPPORT AND CELEBRATE TEAM ACCOMPLISHMENTS

Public ceremonies and celebrations serve the powerful purpose of
bringing people together. They build the social support structures that
are necessary for people to continue to do the challenging work that
extraordinary accomplishments require. Every project milestone is an
opportunity for team members to celebrate what they have accomplished and gather the momentum, energy, and spirit to continue.

Think about a project or assignment you are currently engaged in
(or think about one that you were involved with previously and consider what you might have done in retrospect). Identify project milestones and then brainstorm several fun and meaningful ways for people to celebrate, as a team, reaching these. Later on, get together
with your team, share these ideas, and see which ones they would
love to be part of.

Project milestone	Idea for celebrating this accomplishment as a team

FURTHER REFLECTIONS

- Say "thank you" when you appreciate something that someone has done. Don't be stingy or hesitant about acknowledging the accomplishments of others. Write at least three thank-you notes each week (text messages and emails are okay, but for a real impact try penning a handwritten note). When you receive a thank you on behalf of the group, be sure to share it visibly with everyone in the organization that you can.

- It is OK to ask people how they would like to be recognized, and it is OK to talk with people in your group or organization about how they would like to celebrate with one another. You can't know for sure if you don't ask, and people will always appreciate the personal and personalized touch. Be creative about recognition and rewards. Try photographs, buttons, banners, painted rocks, special T-shirts, hats, rap songs, poems, and the like.

- Be sure to link performance and rewards together. Generally, people repeat behavior that is rewarded and avoid behavior that is punished or ignored. You need to make certain that people know what is expected of them and that you provide feedback on their performance. Be sure to reward only those individuals who meet or exceed the standards.

- Have fun. Sure, leadership is serious work, but who wants to work hard all the time without taking a few moments, every so often, to enjoy one another's company and to laugh? Otherwise, burnout is the result. And don't take *yourself* too seriously either. You are just like everybody else, regardless of position, in that you make mistakes and aren't always at your best. Learn to laugh at yourself and to practice forgiveness for being human.

8

LEADERSHIP IS EVERYONE'S BUSINESS

Throughout this book you've learned about ordinary students who've mobilized others to want to get extraordinary things done in their organizations. The stories have been about men and women from a variety of colleges and universities, public and private, small and large, in the United States and abroad. Not only are the backgrounds of these students all over the map, but the types of organizations in which they experienced their personal-best leadership also represent a full spectrum of collegiate opportunities.

Chances are you haven't heard of any of these exemplary student leaders. They're not making front-page headlines, leading huge student rallies or movements, starring on YouTube, or breaking records as mega-star athletes or entrepreneurs. Rather, they're people who might live next door, study in the next cubicle over, or have lunch in your student union.

We've focused on everyday student leaders because leadership is not about position or title. Leadership is not about organizational power or authority. It's not about being a president, captain, director, chair, editor, CEO, general, or prime minister. It's not about celebrity or wealth. It's not about the family or neighborhood you are born into. And it's definitely not about being a hero. Leadership is about relationships, about credibility, and about what you *do*.

YOU ARE THE MOST IMPORTANT LEADER IN THE ROOM

We regularly ask people in our classes and workshops to share a story about a leader they admire and whose direction they would willingly follow. Virtually everyone we've asked has been able to name at least one leader whose genuine influence they've felt. Sometimes it's a well-known figure—perhaps someone out of the past who changed the course of history. Sometimes it's a contemporary role model who serves as an example of success. Most often, however, it's someone personally close to them who's helped them learn and do things they weren't sure they could achieve—a teacher, coach, parent, relative, or friend.

As a leader, you make a difference. To the people working with you as their leader, there is no more important leader in the organization than you. You are the person people in that group are most likely going to look to for the example of how someone tackles challenging goals, responds to difficult situations, handles crises, deals with setbacks, or resolves ethical dilemmas. It's not someone else. It's *you*. The leaders who have the most influence on people are those who are the *closest* to them.

Whether or not you hold the title of president or chair or captain, using The Five Practices enables you to be an exemplary leader no matter who else is in the room. You have to continually challenge the myth that leadership is about position and power. And once that myth is challenged, people can come to see leadership in a whole new light.

Research demonstrates that student leaders who use The Five Practices of Exemplary Leadership have a positive influence on others in the organization. They are seen as better leaders. People working with them feel more satisfied with their actions and more committed, excited, energized, influential, and powerful.

> **Not being able to do everything is no excuse for not doing everything you can.**
> —Ashleigh Brilliant

Take it from Samantha Morrow, who learned to see leadership in a new light after a year of "position-less" involvement in her college sorority:

Not having a position did not prevent me from leading. . . . As long as I am actively involved and help ensure that things stay organized I can be a leader. I can step in and work for those who are unwilling to do their job. Simply motivating other members and helping where no one will is as much of a leadership position as someone that actually holds a title.

Or listen to Sarah Puddu, who told us how her experience working as an intern in a vision therapy office during her sophomore year in college changed her view of the meaning of leadership:

Although I didn't hold a leadership title I truly saw myself contributing to the well being of the business and the patients. . . .

Whether they were children or adults, they spent much more time with me than with the doctors who ran the office. Their feelings towards their therapy experiences relied on me more than on the doctors. I saw myself contributing to their positive and pleasant experience. . . . I saw myself truly being a leader and contributing to the success of the office, although I did not have a leadership title at the organization. This experience taught me how I didn't have to be the boss there to make a difference.

You see, there's no escape from the fundamental truth introduced at the beginning of the book: *Leadership is everyone's business.* No matter what your position is in your group, you have to take responsibility for the quality of its leadership. You are accountable for the leadership you demonstrate. And because *you* are the most important leader to those closest to you, the only choice you really have is whether or not to be the best leader you can be.

As all the personal-best stories we've collected through the years demonstrate, *leaders make a difference.* If you want to have a significant impact on people, on your community, and on the organizations you're a part of, you'd be wise to invest in learning to become the very best leader you can. But first you must believe—as Sarah, Samantha, and all exemplary leaders do—that a leader lives within each and every one of us.

LEADERSHIP IS LEARNED

The regrettable notion that leadership is reserved for only a very few is reinforced every time someone asks, "Are leaders born or made?" Whenever we're asked this question—which is almost every time we conduct a class or give a speech or lead a workshop—our answer, always offered with a smile, is this: "Yes, of course, all leaders are born. We've never met a leader who wasn't. So are all accountants, artists, athletes, parents, professors, zoologists, you name it." We're all born. What we do with what we have before we die is up to us.

It's just pure myth that only a lucky few can ever understand the intricacies of leadership. Leadership is not a gene, and it's not a secret code that can't be deciphered by ordinary people. The truth is that leadership is *an observable set of skills and abilities* that are useful in any campus, community, or work setting. And any skill can be strengthened, honed, and enhanced, given the motivation and desire, along with practice and feedback, role models, and coaching.

> **I can, therefore I am.**
>
> —Simone Weil

Our evidence is the stories we've read and heard, in over twenty-five years of research, from thousands of ordinary people who've led others to get extraordinary things done. And there are millions more. It's not the absence of leadership potential that inhibits the development of more leaders; it's the persistence of the myth that leadership can't be learned. This haunting myth is a far more powerful deterrent to leadership development than is the nature of the person who aspires to lead or the basics of the leadership process.

Exemplary leaders are leadership myth-busters, and one of our favorite examples is Daren Blonski, who "saw a great need to teach students how to be leaders" while still an undergraduate at his university:

Many students were receiving a world-class education but there was no explicit instruction on how to work with people. With over 200 student groups on campus, few if any of the students leading those groups had had the opportunity to get any formal leadership training. . . . Students needed a framework to think about leadership, and the behavioral tools to practice it.

Daren partnered with student-athlete Will Merchad to start a group called Building Roles. He told us that The Five Practices of Exemplary Leadership were a good foundation for understanding that leadership was everyone's business, and this approach offered the Building Roles group a new perspective on the world of human interaction as they organized seminars, conferences, and other student-led leadership development activities. By the time Daren moved on, Building Roles had trained some two hundred students and received the university's Kaplan Award for excellence in student teamwork.

Daren told us that when he reflected on the experience, he realized that

I learned an important lesson about leadership. If you are going to create something as a leader, it is very important to make sure you are mentoring your next generation of leaders. One of the biggest mistakes that leaders make is that they are so busy mobilizing others that they sometimes forget to make room for others to step forward. Leadership is not simply about mobilizing others to want to realize shared aspirations but it is also about teaching others to mobilize others.

Exemplary leaders like Daren know that the collective task is to liberate the leader in each and every one of an organization's members. Rather than view leadership as an innate set of character traits, it's far healthier and more productive to assume that it's possible for everyone to learn to lead. By assuming that leadership is learnable, you can discover how many good leaders there really are. Somewhere, sometime, the leader within you and each of your group's members may get the call to step forward—for the school, the team, the club, the congregation, the community, the company, or the family. By believing in yourself and your capacity to learn to lead, you make sure you'll be prepared when that call comes.

> *What you see in yourself is*
> *what you see in the world.*
>
> —Afghan proverb

Certainly, no one should mislead people into believing that they can attain unrealistic goals. However, neither should you assume that only a few would ever attain excellence in leadership (or in any other human endeavor). Those who are most successful at bringing out the best in others are those who set achievable "stretch" goals and believe that they have the ability to apply and develop the talents of others.

Effective leaders are constantly learning. They see all experiences as learning experiences, not just those sessions in a formal classroom or workshop. They're constantly looking for ways to improve themselves and their organizations. By reading this book, taking a class or seminar, and engaging in other personal development activities, you're demonstrating a predisposition to lead. Even if some people think that they're not able to learn to lead, *you* must believe that you and they can. That's where it all starts—with your own belief in yourself and in others. If you are to become a better leader, you must first believe that leadership applies to you and that you can be a positive force in the world.

FIRST LEAD YOURSELF

Leadership development is self-development. Engineers have computers; painters, canvas and brushes; musicians, instruments. Leaders have only themselves. The instrument of leadership is the self, and mastery of the art of leadership comes from mastery of the self. Self-development is not about stuffing in a whole bunch of new information or trying out the latest group-process technique. It's about leading out of what is already in your soul. It's about liberating the leader within you. It's about setting yourself free.

The quest for leadership is first an inner quest to discover who you are. Through self-development comes the confidence needed to lead. Self-confidence is really awareness of and faith in your own powers. These powers become clear and strong only as you work to identify and develop them.

> *A bird doesn't sing because it has an answer,*
>
> *it sings because it has a song.*
>
> —Maya Angelou

Learning to lead is about discovering what you care about and value. As you begin this quest toward leadership, you must wrestle with some difficult questions:

- How certain am I of my own convictions and values?

- How will I handle disappointments, mistakes, and setbacks?

- What are my strengths and weaknesses?

- What do I need to do to improve my abilities to move the organization forward?

- How solid is my relationship with my teammates, coworkers, and constituents?

- How can I keep myself motivated and encouraged?

- What keeps me from giving up?

- Am I the right one to be leading at this very moment? Why?

- How much do I understand about what is going on in the organization and the world in which it operates?

- How prepared am I to handle the complex problems that now confront my organization?

- What are my beliefs about how people should behave in this organization?

- Where do I think the organization ought to be headed over the next ten years?

Honest answers to these questions (and to those that arise from them) tell you that you must open yourself to a more global view. The more you know about the world, the easier it is to approach it with assurance. Thus you should seek to learn as much as possible about the forces—political, economic, social, moral, or artistic—that shape that world.

Honest answers also tell you that to become as effective as possible you must improve your understanding of others and build your skills to mobilize people's energies toward higher purposes. To be a leader, you must be interpersonally competent, and you must be able to develop the trust and respect of others. As Maya Babu told us:

> No matter how much experience or education I may possess, effective leadership primarily hinges on gaining and maintaining the trust of those I must lead. Each individual poses a new challenge. I cannot assume that my past will be enough for me to be viewed as a leader. Instead, I must constantly strive to engage and motivate . . . [and] engage my colleagues in a way that builds trust and forms healthy working relationships.

Finally, honest answers to these questions tell you that sometimes liberating the leader within you can be uncomfortable, but in the end, when you answer such questions for yourself you know that what's inside is what you found there and what belongs there. It's not something put inside you by someone else; it's what your true gifts are.

MORAL LEADERSHIP CALLS US TO HIGHER PURPOSES

Leadership practices per se are amoral. But leaders—the men and women who use the practices—are moral or immoral. There's an ethical dimension to leadership that neither leaders nor constituents should take lightly. This is why the discussion of The Five Practices of Exemplary Leadership begins with a focus on clarifying your values—on finding your authentic voice in a particular set of principles and ideals.

These you have to find for yourself and test against others. Attending to moral values will always direct you to higher purposes. As you work to become all you can be, you can start to let go of petty self-interests. As you give back some of what you've been given, you can reconstruct your community. As you serve the values of freedom, justice, equality, caring, and dignity, you can constantly renew the foundations of democracy. As you and each of your constituents take individual responsibility for creating the world of your dreams, you can all participate in leading.

When you clarify the principles that will govern your life and the ends that you will seek, you give purpose to your daily decisions. A personal creed gives you a point of reference for navigating the sometimes-stormy seas of life in any kind of organization. Without such a set of beliefs, your life has no rudder, and you're easily blown about by the winds of fashion. A credo that resolves competing beliefs also leads to personal integrity. A student leader with integrity has one self—at home, at school, at work, with family, with friends, and with colleagues. Leaders without integrity are putting on an act.

> *There are no shortcuts to any place worth going.*
>
> —Beverly Sills

Leaders take people to places they've never been before. But there are no freeways to the future, no paved highways to unknown, unexplored destinations. There's only wilderness. To step out into the unknown, begin with the exploration of the inner territory. The most critical knowledge for everyone—and for leaders especially—turns out to be self-knowledge.

HUMILITY IS THE ANTIDOTE TO HUBRIS

There's a catch: There's absolutely no way that we can say that The Five Practices will work everywhere, all of the time, with everyone. We know for certain that there's a much greater probability that they will, but there's no ironclad, money-back guarantee. In addition, you will never find, in historic or present times, even one example of a leader who controlled every aspect of the environment. And you'll never find an example of a leader who enlisted 100 percent of the possible constituency in even the most compelling of future possibilities.

And there's still another catch: any leadership practice can become destructive. Virtues can become vices. There's a point at which each of The Five Practices, taken to extremes, can lead you astray.

Although clarifying values and setting an example are essential to modeling, an obsession with being seen as a role model can lead to being too focused on your own voice and your way of doing things. It can cause you to discount others' views and be closed to feedback. It can push you into isolation for fear of losing privacy or being "found out"; it can also cause you to be more concerned with style than with substance.

Being forward-looking and communicating a clear and common vision of the future are practices that set leaders apart from other credible people. Yet a singular focus on one vision of the future can blind you to other possibilities as well as to the realities of the present. It can cause you to miss the exciting possibilities that are just out of your sight or make you hang on just a little too long to an old, tired, and out-of-date technology. Exploiting your powers of inspiration can cause others to surrender their will. Your own energy, enthusiasm, and charm may be so magnetic that others don't think for themselves.

Challenging the process is essential to promoting innovation and progressive change. Seizing the initiative and taking risks are necessary actions for learning and continuous improvement. But take this to extremes and you can create needless turmoil, confusion, and paranoia. Routines are important, and if you seldom give people an opportunity to gain confidence and competence they'll lose their motivation to try new things. Change for change's sake can be just as demoralizing as complacency.

Collaboration and teamwork are essential to getting extraordinary things done in today's world. But an overreliance on collaboration and trust may reflect an avoidance of critical decisions or cause errors in judgment. It may be a way of *not* taking charge when the situation requires. Delegating power and responsibility can become a way of dumping too much on others when they're not fully prepared to handle it.

Personal recognition and group celebration create the spirit and momentum that can carry a group forward even during the toughest of challenges. At the same time, if you constantly worry about who should be recognized and when you should celebrate, you can become too focused on being a gregarious minstrel. You can lose sight of the mission because you're having so much fun; so consumed by all the perks and pleasures that you forget the purpose of it all.

Then there's the treachery of hubris. It's fun to be a leader, gratifying to have influence, and exhilarating to have scores of people cheering your every word. In many subtle and not-so-subtle ways, it's easy to be seduced by power and importance. All evil leaders have been infected with the disease of hubris, becoming bloated with an exaggerated sense of self and pursuing their own sinister ends. How then to avoid it?

> *We come nearest to the great when*
>
> *we are great in humility.*
>
> —Rabindranath Tagore

Humility is the only way to resolve the conflicts and contradictions of leadership. You can avoid excessive pride only if you recognize that you're human and need the help of others. Exemplary student leaders know that they can't do it alone, and they act accordingly. They lack the pride and pretense displayed by many leaders who succeed in the short term but leave behind a weak organization that fails to remain viable after their departure. Instead, with self-effacing humor and generous and sincere credit to others, humble leaders inspire higher and higher levels of performance.

Nothing in our research hints that leaders should be perfect. Leaders aren't saints. They're human beings, full of human flaws and failings. They trip up. They get off track. They make mistakes. Perhaps the very best advice we can give all aspiring leaders is to remain humble and unassuming—to always remain open and full of wonder.

LEADERSHIP IS IN THE MOMENT

Sometimes we imagine leadership to be something majestic—about grand visions, about world-changing initiatives, about transforming the lives of millions. All these are noble possibilities, but real leadership occurs one moment at a time. Real leadership approaches every interaction and every situation as an opportunity to lead.

In reflecting on his journey to becoming a better leader as a young entrepreneur, Sergey Nikiforov answered his own question "Where do I start becoming a better leader?" with a simple yet profound realization: "I found that every day I had an opportunity to make a small difference."

The task can feel daunting at times, he told us, but how you respond in each of those moments is the ultimate difference between being a leader or not:

> I found that . . . I could have listened better, I could have been more positive toward people, I could have said "thank you" more often, I could have . . . the list just went on.
>
> At first, I was a bit overwhelmed with the discovery of how many opportunities I had in a single day to act as a better leader. But as I have gotten to put these ideas into practice I have been pleasantly surprised by how much improvement I have been able to make by being more conscientious and intentional about acting as a leader.

Sergey has nailed it. Each day provides countless chances to make a difference. The chance may come in a private conversation with a teammate or in a meeting with fellow volunteers on a community service project. It may come over the family dinner table or in the student cafeteria. It may come when you're on the platform speaking on the future of your organization, or when you're listening to a friend talk about a current conflict with a classmate. There are many moments each day, as exemplary leaders like Sergey point out, when you can choose to lead, and many moments each day when you can choose to make a difference. Each of these moments serves up the prospect of contributing to a lasting legacy.

THE SECRET TO SUCCESS IN LIFE

Constituents look for leaders who demonstrate an enthusiastic and genuine belief in the capacity of others, who strengthen people's will, who supply the means to achieve, and who express optimism for the future. Constituents want leaders who remain passionate despite obstacles and setbacks. In uncertain times, leaders with a positive, confident, can-do approach to life are desperately needed.

Never stop believing in dreaming, and
never stop dreaming of believing. That is what
gives us hope, and what keeps us alive.

—Unknown

Leaders must keep hope alive, even in the most difficult of times. Without hope there can be no courage—and this is not the time or place for the timid. This is the time and place for optimism, imagination, enthusiasm, and initiative. Leaders must summon their will if they are to mobilize the personal and organizational resources to triumph against the odds. Hope is essential to achieving the highest levels of performance. Hope enables people to transcend the difficulties of today and envision the potentialities of tomorrow. Hope enables people to bounce back even after being stressed, stretched, and depressed. Hope enables people to find the will and the way to unleash greatness.

And yet, hope is not all. There's still one more final leadership lesson that we have learned. It's the secret to success in life.

When we began our study of leadership bests we were fortunate to cross paths with then U.S. Army Major General John H. Stanford. We knew that he had grown up poor, that he failed sixth grade but went on to graduate from Penn State University on an ROTC scholarship, that he survived multiple military tours in both Korea and Vietnam, that he headed up the Military Traffic Management Command for the U.S. Army during the Persian Gulf War, that he was highly decorated, and that the loyalty of his troops was extraordinary. After retiring from the military John took on important leadership roles in local government (in Atlanta, Georgia) and public school education (in Seattle, Washington).

All that was impressive, but it was his answer to one of our interview questions that was a significant influence on our own understanding of leadership. We asked John how he'd go about developing leaders, whether in colleges and universities, in the military, in government, in the non-profit sector, or in private business. He replied,

> When anyone asks me that question, I tell them I have the secret to success in life. The secret to success is to stay in love. Staying in love gives you the fire to ignite other people, to see inside other people, to have a greater desire to get things done than other people. A person who is not in love doesn't really feel the kind of excitement that helps them to get ahead and to lead others and to achieve. I don't know any other fire, any other thing in life that is more exhilarating and is more positive a feeling than love is.

"Staying in love" isn't the answer we expected to get from anyone, at least not when we began our study of leadership more than twenty-five years ago. But after years of interviews and case analyses, it finally dawned on us how many leaders—young and old, new and experienced—used the word *love* freely when talking about their own motivations to lead.

The best-kept secret of successful leaders is love: staying in love with leading, with the people who do the work of the organization; staying in love with their organization's products and services, and with those who honor the organization by using them. It is hard to imagine getting up each day and working real hard if you don't put your heart into your work and your work into your heart. Leadership, when all is said and done, is not an affair of the head. Leadership is an affair of the heart.

REVIEW AND PRACTICE

You've come full circle, from beginning with finding your voice, to putting your values and visions into action through the minds and hearts of others, to remembering that it was never all about you, or that just because you believe deeply and sincerely, that will be sufficient to guarantee success. And still the truth that can't be escaped is that you matter; you make a difference. Leadership doesn't begin until you believe in yourself so much that you are willing to give voice and take action even if at the beginning the only person following you is yourself.

Leadership is learned. No one, including leaders, gets it right the first time around. Experience is the best teacher, and while we reflect on our own experiences we can also learn much from the experiences of both those who have come before us as well as those around us. Recognizing that learning never ends—that you don't know it all—is one potent antidote for the disease of hubris. Listening, being open to new and different experiences, and learning from others are the ingredients for humility.

There are no shortages of opportunities to make a difference. Leadership matters at the front door, shop floor, front line, and first level every bit as much as it does in the corner office, executive suite, board room, and corporate officer ranks. Leadership is an attitude and a sense of responsibility as necessary for individual and organizational success on college campuses as it is in corporations, communities, and public offices. Leadership is everyone's business.

Here are some further steps for this leg of your leadership journey.

I. THE LEGACY THAT I WILL LEAVE

Imagine that it's one year after your project or assignment was successfully concluded. (It doesn't really make a difference if you are thinking of something you are now involved with or it's one you can see yourself working on in the future.) You overhear several people talking about the legacy you've left as a result of how the project or assignment was handled. What are the things you hope to hear them say?

1.

2.

3.

4.

5.

What are the sorts of inputs that you will need to pay attention to in the here and now if you intend to have this kind of impact?

1.

2.

3.

4.

5.

II. INTERVIEW ABOUT MY LEADERSHIP

You can be certain that one of the questions employers will ask you in any job interview (right after college or even fifty years later!) is about your leadership experience. Make a few notes to yourself about how you will respond to the following questions. Better yet, get together with a classmate and run through a mock interview with one another using these questions to get ready for that fateful interview.

- Tell me about a time you were in charge of a group of people. What did you like about being in charge? What didn't you like?

- Tell me about something you achieved as a group leader.

- Tell me about something you achieved as a group member.

- Give me an example of your ability to facilitate progressive change within a group you have been involved with.

- How have you been able to get a group of people to work together as a team?

- What motivates you to put forth extra effort? Describe a situation in which you did so.

- How would you evaluate your ability to deal with conflict?

- Describe a creative solution that you have used to solve a problem.

- Describe something you have accomplished that shows your initiative.

- When is the last time you took a risk, and what happened?

- Tell me about a situation you have faced that required strong communication skills.

- What qualities should a successful leader possess?

III. MY LEADERSHIP EDITORIAL

Leadership is a journey, not a destination. The race, for leaders, is one that doesn't have a finish line. And the process of leadership is just as applicable whether you are sitting in a classroom, on an athletic field, or in a residence hall, chapter house, community service engagement, or the student senate chambers.

Having completed this book on leadership, and after reviewing your own experiences as well as the experiences of others (both inside and outside of your classroom), write an editorial for your campus newspaper about what you think it takes for a student to be a leader on your campus. What advice would you give students wanting to be leaders based on your experiences and research?

FURTHER REFLECTIONS

- Start keeping a leadership notebook or diary. Take a few moments of quiet reflection each day and ask yourself, "How consistent were my actions and my values today?" Note what you learned about yourself and from others, and what you can do more of or differently in the days ahead. There is no real substitute for learning by doing.

- Practice, practice, practice. People who practice more often are more likely to become experts at what they do than those who don't practice. Because leadership is a skill, it can be improved with practice, and practice is essential to learning. Similarly, seek opportunities to take on a leadership role. Make speeches. Be a mentor. Coach a team. Volunteer to head projects for your dorm, apartment, class, or club, and don't forget about the opportunities in the community around campus.

- Make a mistake. If you are not making any mistakes, you are not learning; you are only doing what you already know how to do. Keep in mind that failure is always an option. Not everything you are going to do or attempt as a leader is going to work out as you intended. Indeed, if you're not willing to fail at what you do, you'll never become great. It's your point of view that makes a difference. Ask yourself, "What can I learn from this experience?" If you have to fall, fall forward.

- Have a conversation about courage. Take the time to explore the role that courage plays in your life: What adversities in your life are causing you great hardship and suffering? What are you most afraid of? How ready are you to sacrifice and suffer? Reflecting on these questions will enrich your understanding of courage, open up your capacity to act with courage, and possibly provide the spark for leaving your mark.

APPENDIX

The Student Leadership Practices Inventory

We have validated that the actions that make up The Five Practices of Exemplary Leadership can be translated into behavioral statements relevant to students. The result was the Student Leadership Practices Inventory (SLPI), which enables students to assess their behaviors and use this feedback to improve their leadership abilities.

The SLPI lends quantitative evidence to the qualitative data provided by personal-best leadership case studies. If these were the practices of student leaders when they were at their personal best, then those people who are engaged in The Five Practices of Exemplary Student Leadership should be more effective than those who are not. Similarly, the small groups, work teams, clubs, and organizations characterized by student leaders engaging in The Five Practices should be more motivated and productive. Their commitment and satisfaction levels should be greater when people report being led by student leaders whose behaviors match up with The Five Practices of Exemplary Student Leadership.

Indeed, these are precisely the findings from our empirical studies, as well as the conclusions from research projects conducted by hundreds of other scholars and doctoral students (summaries of which can be viewed at www.theleadershipchallenge.com). The Five Practices of Exemplary Student Leadership make a difference. Consider just a few of the revealing findings documented by these studies:

- Student LPI scores of effective fraternity and sorority chapter presidents are significantly higher than those reported for less effective fraternity and sorority chapter presidents.

- New students' satisfaction with their on-campus orientation experience is significantly correlated with the extent to which they report their orientation advisors are engaged in The Five Practices as measured by the SLPI.

- The effectiveness ratings given to residential hall assistants by directors of residential living are directly correlated with the SLPI scores of the residential hall assistants.

- The greater the frequency with which residential hall assistants are engaging in The Five Practices, the more the students living on their floors report being satisfied with their living situations.

- The SLPI scores are higher for those elected student government leaders seen by their peers as effective and credible than for those reported as less effective and credible.

Findings such as these have been noted across a variety of campus settings and locations, as well as for students from a vast array of both formal and informal organizations. Moreover, the ability to engage in The Five Practices of Exemplary Student Leadership has generally not been found to be related to academic achievement (GPA), gender, ethnic background, or personality variable, or to following a particular course of study or major. The desire to lead and make a difference is the spark that ignites the flame of leadership within.

DESCRIPTION OF THE STUDENT LPI

The SLPI consists of thirty statements that address the essential behaviors found when students report being at their personal best as leaders. In addition to a "Self" version, the "Observer" version allows for 360-degree feedback from constituents in order to provide a balanced picture of leadership behaviors and constructive discussion of ways to improve.

Responses are marked on a five-point scale, with behavioral anchors. For each statement, respondents indicate the frequency with which the particular behavior is engaged in by the individual. Responses range from 1, indicating "rarely or seldom," to 5, indicating "very frequently." Each of the five leadership practice measures comprises six statements. Scoring software provides feedback along a number of dimensions, including comparisons by respondent category or relationship with the normative database, rankings by frequency, and variances between "Self" and "Observer" scores.

The SLPI Student Workbook provides helpful interpretive feedback and space to make plans for improvement in each leadership practice assessed. There are sections on how to "make sense" of the feedback, identifying both personal strengths and areas for further development, as well as advice on how to collect additional information and discuss the data with constituents. The Student Leadership Planner, a companion piece to the SLPI Student Workbook, presents a process for continuous leadership development over time and includes numerous specific tips and strategies for learning how to be a more effective leader and continuing to develop and hone one's leadership capabilities.

Ordering and other information about the SLPI can be found at the back of this book and at www.studentlpi.com.

PSYCHOMETRIC PROPERTIES OF THE STUDENT LPI

The SLPI has been field-tested and proven reliable in identifying the behaviors that make a difference in student leaders' effectiveness. The SLPI takes about ten minutes to complete. To generate 360-degree feedback, one can gather responses from an advisor (or supervisor, manager, director), coworkers or peers, or direct reports. With data from over ten thousand respondents, the SLPI has demonstrated sound psychometric properties. The most current information on the research supporting the Student LPI can be found at www.theleadershipchallenge.com.

Reliability of the Student LPI

The internal reliability (the extent to which items in a scale are associated with one another) of the SLPI is strong. All five leadership practices have internal reliability scores (as measured statistically with Cronbach's alpha) that are generally between .70 and .85. Test-retest reliability scores are very robust and routinely in the .90-plus range, with little significant social desirability bias reported. Various demographic factors—such as year in school, major, GPA, gender, and ethnicity—do not play a significant role in explaining leadership behaviors.

Validity of the Student LPI

Validity is the answer to the question: "So what difference do scores on the Student LPI make?" This question is addressed empirically by looking at how SLPI scores are correlated with other measures, typically of important outcomes such as satisfaction, productivity, team spirit, pride, reputation, and the like. To minimize self-report biases, responses from the Student LPI-Observer are used in these analyses, rather than responses from the Student LPI-Self.

The evaluations of student leaders by their constituents (chapter officers, teammates, volunteers, advisors, and so on) are consistently and directly correlated with assessments of the extent to which these leaders engage in The Five Practices of Exemplary Student Leadership. In other words, student leaders are consistently evaluated more favorably (across a number of dimensions) by their constituents as they are seen as engaging more frequently in The Five Practices. This is a strong normative statement. However, studies also show that leadership can be learned. Any student leader who wants to make a difference, gets good coaching and feedback, and puts the leadership practices to regular use can significantly improve his or her ability and comfort level engaging in The Five Practices and associated leadership behaviors.

ACKNOWLEDGMENTS

One of the great joys of publishing a book is the opportunity to work with scores of talented, dedicated, and inspiring people. While the tasks of writing are often lonely and tedious, the pleasures of interacting with our colleagues are always fun and uplifting. We are profoundly grateful to them, and we will never let an opportunity go by to say "thank you" to all who have joined us on this journey.

Thank you to the thousands of students we've worked with over the years. You inspire us and bring us hope. You give us immense confidence that our future is held in capable hands and generous hearts.

As always, thank you to our immediate loved ones—Tae and Nick, Jackie and Amanda. You bring great joy into our lives and make the times we have together forever memorable. We have witnessed—and experienced—your extraordinary feats of leadership, and from you we have learned more than we can ever share.

We would also like to thank some very special people who were especially helpful on this project. Leslie Stephen, as she has now done with several of our manuscripts, worked closely with us to transform concepts, research, and examples into prose and practical ideas. Leslie, you are a gem! From the start, Erin Null championed this project with her colleagues at Jossey-Bass, an imprint of Wiley. She moved us forward with caring leadership and a gracious guiding hand. The genius of Lisa Shannon gets applied in all of our Jossey-Bass and Pfeiffer adventures, and we always love to work with her. We look forward to many more projects with

Lisa in the future! Karyn Bechtel, Daren Blonski, Amanda Crowell Itliong, Amelia Klawon, David Klawon, Laura Osteen, and Jackie Schmidt-Posner all provided timely, informative, and challenging feedback on early drafts of the manuscript. Their sage advice and wise counsel improved both the substance and tone of the final version. We're deeply appreciative of their insights and nudging.

Finally, a special round of applause for all those students whose stories, experiences, lessons, and wisdom make up the centerpieces of *The Student Leadership Challenge.* Thank you for what you've accomplished and for who you are. And many thanks to scores of other students who have shared their experiences with us, even if we couldn't put everyone's stories into this book. We know that the readers of this book will become better leaders as a result of reading the lessons of your experiences.

We wrote this book, as we have each of our books, in order to liberate the leader that lies within each of us. That's our mission and our passion. Each and every one of us matters. Each and every one of us makes a difference. The real challenge for all of us is to continue to make the difference we intended. Live your life forward.

ABOUT THE AUTHORS

Jim Kouzes grew up in the Washington, D.C., area, where he was deeply influenced by the political climate of the nation's capital. Jim was one of the youngest boys in the country to earn the rank of Eagle Scout, and as a result at age fifteen he was selected to serve in John F. Kennedy's Honor Guard. Jim believes it was on that day—January 20, 1961—with the dynamic new president standing directly in front of him, that he was first inspired to dedicate himself to a lifelong study of leadership.

Jim attended Fairfax High School, where he played football for two years and was second trumpet in the high school orchestra for four years. He was active in forensics and theater, performing in both the junior and senior plays. As a Key Club member he was responsible for bringing the first AFS exchange student to the school. His family hosted Aaro Vakkuri of Finland, and the experience of living with someone from a different country sparked a keen interest in global affairs and directed him in his choice of international relations as his college major. While attending Michigan State University in the volatile period of the early sixties, Jim served in student government and worked on the committee that brought social activists to campus to educate students on the issues of the day, particularly civil rights and the war in Vietnam. He graduated with honors (bachelor's in political science), and then fulfilled a dream ignited in 1961 to serve in the Peace Corps. He was a volunteer in Turkey for two years, from 1967 to 1969.

Returning to the United States in 1969, Jim took his first job with the Community Action Program Training Institute, a War on Poverty initiative.

He continued his community service work with the poor and disadvantaged, primarily in the South and Southwest of the United States. It was here that he got his first opportunity to train leaders, taking him down a path that became his life's work. His career in academic administration followed at the University of Texas School of Social Work and then San Jose State University, where he founded the Joint Center for Human Services Development. He was one of the founders in the San Francisco Bay Area chapter of the Organization Development Network. Jim moved to Santa Clara University to head up their Executive Development Center, and after eight years in that position he went on to serve for twelve years as president, CEO, and chairman of the Tom Peters Company. He is currently the Dean's Executive Professor of Leadership, Leavey School of Business, at Santa Clara University.

Not only is Jim a highly regarded leadership scholar and an experienced executive, but also he has been cited by the *Wall Street Journal* as one of the twelve best executive educators in the United States. In 2006 Jim was presented with the Golden Gavel, the highest honor awarded by Toastmasters International. Jim's wife, Tae, is an executive coach and partner with him in several leadership programs. His stepson, Nicholas, is currently a student at the University of California, Davis, attending on a tennis scholarship and playing on their NCAA Division I tennis team. Jim can be reached at jim@kouzes.com.

Barry Posner graduated from Pomona High School in southern California, where he was captain of the tennis team and active in speech and debate (reaching the national finals in oratorical interpretation and earning his double-ruby in the National Forensic League). At the University of California, Santa Barbara, he was sophomore class president, representative-at-large on the Associated Students Legislative Council, and president of his fraternity chapter.

After receiving his bachelor's degree in political science (with honors), Barry worked as a regional director for Sigma Phi Epsilon fraternity and was subsequently elected as the youngest member—and first-ever candidate from the floor of the Conclave—to be elected to their national board of directors, on which he served for eight years. At The Ohio State University, where he received his master's degree in public administration, Barry did an internship with the director of the OSU Student Unions. He received his doctoral degree in organizational behavior and administrative theory at the University of Massachusetts, Amherst. While at UMass, he was the chapter counselor for the local Sig Ep chapter, and he and his wife, Jackie, served as house parents residing in one of the campus sorority chapters.

Barry has been on the management faculty at Santa Clara University for over thirty years; currently he serves as dean of the Leavey School of Business and professor of leadership. He has received numerous teaching and innovation awards, including the Extraordinary Faculty Award (several times) and the President's Distinguished Faculty Award. An internationally renowned scholar and educator, Barry is author or coauthor of more than a hundred research and practitioner-focused articles. He serves on the editorial review boards for *Leadership and Organizational Development, Leadership Review,* and *The International Journal of Servant-Leadership.*

Barry currently sits on the boards of directors of the San Jose Repertory Theatre, EMQ Family & Children Services, and Advanced Energy. He has served previously on the board of the American Institute of Architects (AIA), Junior Achievement of Silicon Valley and Monterey Bay, Public Allies, Big Brothers/Big Sisters of Santa Clara County, the Center for Excellence in Nonprofits, and several start-up companies.

He is a warm and engaging conference speaker and dynamic workshop facilitator. His wife, Jackie, is the interim director of the Haas Center for

Public Service (Stanford University). Their daughter, Amanda, recently graduated from the University of Chicago with master's degrees in social work and public policy and is working with After School Matters, a city of Chicago initiative. You can reach Barry at bposner@scu.edu.

Together, Jim and Barry have written nine books and dozens of articles and contributed chapters on leadership. *The Leadership Challenge* has sold over 1.6 million copies and been translated into seventeen languages. It has received numerous awards, among them the James A. Hamilton Hospital Administrators' Book Award, the Critics' Choice Award, Amazon.com Best Business Books of the Year, and has been a *Business-Week* best-seller. They also developed the highly acclaimed Leadership Practices Inventory (LPI), a 360-degree questionnaire for assessing leadership behavior, which is one of the most widely used leadership assessment instruments in the world. More than three hundred fifty doctoral dissertations and academic research projects have been based on The Five Practices of Exemplary Leadership model.

Jim and Barry were named Management/Leadership Educators of the Year by the International Management Council. This honor puts them in the company of Ken Blanchard, Stephen R. Covey, Peter Drucker, Edward Deming, Frances Hesselbein, Lee Iacocca, Rosabeth Moss Kanter, Norman Vincent Peale, and Tom Peters. In the book *Coaching for Leadership* they were listed among the nation's top leadership educators, and in 2007 they were named among the Top 75 Best in Leadership Development by *Leadership Excellence*.

Jim and Barry are frequent conference speakers, and each has conducted leadership development programs for scores of colleges and universities, including Stanford, University of Dayton, Florida State, Drake University, and University of Cincinnati. They have also worked with hundreds of organizations around the globe, including Apple, Applied

Materials, AT&T, Australia Post, Bank of America, Bose, Cisco Systems, Community Leadership Association, Conference Board of Canada, Consumers Energy, Dell Computer, Deloitte Touche, Dorothy Wylie Nursing Leadership Institute, Egon Zehnder International, Federal Express, Gymboree, Hewlett-Packard, IBM, Jobs DR-Singapore, Johnson & Johnson, Kaiser Foundation Health Plans and Hospitals, L. L. Bean, Lawrence Livermore National Labs, Lucile Packard Children's Hospital, Merck, Mervyn's, Motorola, Network Appliance, Northrop Grumman, Roche Bioscience, Siemens, Standard Aero, Sun Microsystems, 3M, Toyota, United Way, USAA, Verizon, VISA, and The Walt Disney Company.

More information about the work of Jim Kouzes and Barry Posner, their research, and the family of products and services related to The Leadership Challenge can be found at www.theleadershipchallenge.com.

INDEX